# HANS FREI AND KARL BARTH

# Hans Frei and Karl Barth

## DIFFERENT WAYS OF READING SCRIPTURE

David E. Demson

WILLIAM B. EERDMANS PUBLISHING COMPANY
GRAND RAPIDS, MICHIGAN / CAMBRIDGE, U.K.

© 1997 Wm. B. Eerdmans Publishing Co.
255 Jefferson Ave. S.E., Grand Rapids, Michigan 49503 /
P.O. Box 163, Cambridge CB3 9PU U.K.

Printed in the United States of America

02 01 00 99 98 97     7 6 5 4 3 2 1


**Library of Congress Cataloging-in-Publication Data**

Demson, David E.
    Hans Frei and Karl Barth: different ways of reading scripture /
    David E. Demson.
        p.    cm.
    Includes bibliographical references.
    ISBN 0-8028-4168-6 (pbk.: alk. paper)
    1.  Frei, Hans W. — Contributions in Biblical hermeneutics.
2. Barth, Karl, 1886-1968 — Contributions in Biblical hermeneutics.
3. Bible — Criticism, interpretation, etc. — History — 20th century.
I. Title.
BS500.D465  1997
220.6′092′2 — dc20                                    96-43911
                                                        CIP

# Contents

# *Preface*

Hans Frei has written about biblical hermeneutics with such learning, cogency, modesty, and grace that he has gained a wide and respectful audience. He is, by any account, a major figure in the field of biblical hermeneutics. And Karl Barth, as far as I know, has undertaken more biblical exposition than any other major theologian of the century.

It is well known that Frei greatly respected Barth's work. One might properly assume that Frei gathered clues about the procedures for reading Scripture from Barth's expository work. Indeed, Frei says as much. But that is not to say that Barth's and Frei's respective procedures for reading Scripture are the same. In fact, at the conclusion of this book, I will seek to make clear their differences.

While this study is descriptive, then, it is not only that. For in comparing and contrasting Barth's and Frei's respective readings of Scripture, I was confronted with Frei's account of an unsubstitutable Savior whose presence is indefinite, and Barth's account of an unsubstitutable Savior whose presence is definite. Since Barth provides an extensive exposition of Scripture's account of the definiteness of Christ's presence, I could only conclude that there is a lacuna in Frei's reading of Scripture. And since, for both Barth and Frei, the procedures for reading Scripture are governed by the patterns and procedures embedded in Scripture, the lacuna in Frei's reading of Scripture affects his hermeneutics.

In assessing the hermeneutical difference between Barth and Frei, and being indebted to both, I have sought to be impartial; but I have not been neutral.

# *Beginning Notes*

1. Barth capitalizes the pronouns that refer to Jesus or to God. Frei does not. While I have kept the original capitalization in quotes, I have used lowercase letters throughout my text.

2. Barth does not use the terms that he employs to describe Jesus' relationship with the apostles with fixed consistency. He uses *Einsetzung* for what is translated in the *Church Dogmatics* as "appointment." Usually he uses *Berufung* for "calling" and *Auftrag* or *Befehl* for "commission." But he also sometimes uses *Berufung* for what, in its context, has the sense of appointment and *Einsetzung* where we might expect *Berufung*. In this study, following a terminological consistency that Barth does not, I use the word *appointment* where Barth is referring to Jesus' gathering of the Twelve during his Galilean ministry, the word *calling* where Barth is referring to Jesus' upholding of the disciples by his intercession for them, and the word *commission* where Barth is referring to Jesus' sending of the apostles in the power of his exaltation. These terms describe a material differentiation of one and the same reality.

3. As Barth uses the terms "apostles" and "disciples" interchangeably, so do I here.

4. In this book I repeatedly use the phrase "the appointment, calling, and commissioning of the apostles" as well as its alternate, "the gathering, upholding, and sending of the apostles." Since this threefold movement is decisive in Barth's understanding of the unity, interpretation, and inspiration of Scripture, an attempt to avoid the repetition, for stylistic reasons, seemed inadvisable. Very occasionally, I use the

phrase "threefold chosenness" as an alternate, and twice simply "calling" as an alternate.

5. The numbers in parentheses in the text refer in the case of Frei to *The Identity of Jesus Christ: The Hermeneutical Bases of Dogmatic Theology* (Philadelphia: Fortress Press, 1975) and in the case of Barth to the *Church Dogmatics* (Edinburgh: T. & T. Clark, 1956-69), the particular volume of which being indicated in a footnote or in the text.

6. In this book I quote Barth's phrase "lost and defecting Israel." When Barth uses this phrase, he almost always uses it as the middle term between the first term "lost and defecting apostolate" and the last term "lost and defecting humankind." Without this context the phrase can be easily misconstrued.

# Introduction

In *The Identity of Jesus Christ,* Hans Frei observes that the gospel story makes constant reference to Jesus' obedience to his mission. This emphasis indicates that the center of Jesus' person is not in himself but in relation to the events of his life and the persons he encountered.[1] In this observation Frei is at no distance from Karl Barth, who reminds his reader that Jesus himself is called "apostle" in Hebrews 3:1, which is a succinct way of summarizing the New Testament emphasis on Jesus' mission.[2] And it is evident that both Frei and Barth can say that Jesus' mission is to enact humans' good on their behalf.

But a distance does open between Frei and Barth. For while both say that Jesus and Jesus alone fulfills his mission of reconciling to God all creatures, Barth goes on to emphasize that Jesus does not will to remain alone, but chooses others to participate actively in his mission of making effective that reconciliation among all creatures. While Jesus alone justifies and sanctifies all creatures and is alone *the* light, he chooses others to be a corresponding light. And these others in the first place are the disciples, the Twelve. It is not the case, though, that Jesus first enacts the good of humans on their behalf, accomplishing the reconciliation of all creatures, and *then* chooses his witnesses to proclaim this enactment as the content of their message. Rather, during the course of this enactment or accomplishment he appoints and calls them, and

1. Hans W. Frei, *The Identity of Jesus Christ* (Philadelphia: Fortress Press, 1975), p. 107.
2. Karl Barth, *Church Dogmatics,* II/2 (Edinburgh: T. & T. Clark, 1957), p. 432.

only the commissioning or sending of them waits upon his accomplishment of reconciliation and his announcement of it. Ingredient in Jesus' identity are his appointment, calling, and commissioning of the Twelve.[3]

While Barth would concur with Frei that the only presence of Christ *now* that may be properly conceived is his presence in the identity that he enacted and that is manifested in the gospel story, Barth speaks of Jesus' enacted and manifested identity as that of the One who appoints, calls, and sends disciples. Jesus' appointment, calling, and sending of disciples today is their inclusion in his choosing of the Twelve. In terms of hermeneutics, this offers a clue to the relation between present witness and the witness of the New Testament. Perhaps even more important for hermeneutics, the choosing of the Twelve is a clue to how we are to explicate the New Testament texts themselves.

What schema does Barth employ to draw together or make continuous the appointment, calling, and commissioning of the Twelve? These are not three independent acts connected only by their sequence and therefore to be interrelated in consideration of the whole, such as by a literary consideration of them. A schema from Barth's ecclesiology gives every appearance of being materially and formally adequate. Jesus gathered, upheld, and sent the twelve disciples.[4] He gathered them to participate actively in his mission, so the gathering anticipates their sending, as the appointment texts clearly demonstrate (e.g., "I will make you fishers of men," Matt. 5:19). They are sent to teach and preach and make disciples and baptize. With what power? Jesus calls humans, and first of all the disciples, out of sin and into the freedom of new life — in the power of the accomplished reconciliation. It is as forgiven sinners that the apostles preach and teach.[5] Apart from the forgiveness of sins and entry into new life as the fulfillment of Israel's history — accomplished by Christ — the apostles have nothing to preach and teach. There is no commission to the apostles apart from their calling to acknowledge, recognize, and confess their own forgiveness of sins and entry into new life, and to proclaim that this same forgiveness and newness is granted to all whom they encounter.

3. It is also the case that ingredient in Jesus' identity is his relation to Israel — of which both Frei and Barth take account — and, also, at the margin, his relation to the Gentile world, of which Barth takes account and Frei makes mention.

4. *Church Dogmatics,* IV/1, p. 643; IV/2, p. 614; IV/3 (second half), p. 681 (Edinburgh: T. & T. Clark, 1956, 1958, 1962).

5. Barth makes "upholding" and "calling" very nearly synonyms. This will be examined in what follows.

There is nothing in Barth's theology that would call into question Frei's account of Jesus' obedience, his existence in power and powerlessness, and in its transition from the one to the other. Nor does Barth's theology veto the account Frei gives of the relation of Jesus and God in terms of Frei's schema of supplantation and identification, even though Barth's Christology is developed much more explicitly in terms of the history of christological dogma. But what Barth includes and Frei leaves out of account in their respective descriptions of the New Testament's depiction of Jesus' identity is Jesus' gathering, upholding, and sending of the apostles.

Before placing side by side Barth's exposition of the New Testament accounts of Jesus' singling out the apostles and Frei's exposition of the Gospels according to his intention-action schema, I will compare their respective accounts of the stages of the gospel story. This comparison will anticipate Frei's inattention to and Barth's concentration on Jesus' making disciples of the Twelve.

# 1 The Stages of the Gospel Story

Frei's exposition of the gospel story is more nearly a literary analysis.[1] In the first stage of the story, the birth and infancy narratives, Jesus is a stylized figure identified wholly in terms of the people Israel. In Frei's exposition this prepares the way for a reversal in the final stage, in which the unsubstitutable Jesus, who has enacted his identity and as such is manifest as the presence of God's action, is the climactic summation of Israel's history and mission.

For Barth, who also speaks of a three-stage gospel story, the first stage consists of Jesus' Galilean ministry.[2] Barth emphasizes that it occurs within the wider and narrower circles of his disciples, the multitudes, and (on the margin) the spiritual and political rulers of the people. Jesus is within these circles, and yet his words and acts are in antithesis to the whole being and thinking and willing of these men. This antithesis is not effectively breached in this stage. Even in his general account of the gospel story, Barth emphasizes Jesus' relationship with the disciples. In stage one, he is the Judge, as Teacher, of the disciples (and the others).

Frei's description of the second stage (nearly coincident with what Barth regards as the first stage) has it commencing with Jesus' baptism and ending with his journey to Jerusalem. Jesus is more nearly an individual in this stage than in the first. He performs mighty deeds. He proclaims the kingdom of God and teaches its manner of life. Yet

1. *Identity,* chap. 12.
2. *C.D.* IV/1, pp. 224-28.

1

he is still a representative figure — he represents the kingdom he proclaims. Thus, while Jesus begins to emerge as an unsubstitutable individual, he is also a stylized representative figure. In his account of this stage Frei leaves out of account Jesus' transference of his mission to the apostles; indeed, he does not explicitly mention the disciples — they are only implicitly present as hearers (with others) of Jesus' proclamation and as witnesses (with others) of his deeds.

In Barth's exposition the second stage begins either with Jesus' entry into Jerusalem or with the scene in the Garden of Gethsemane and ends with Jesus' burial. In this sequence Barth notes, as does Frei, a strict unity of subject matter and an unbroken sequence of events. Beginning with the scene in the Garden of Gethsemane, there are very few sayings of Jesus and no actions of Jesus at all. Here Jesus is object, not subject, of what happens. His speech is largely silence, his work that of suffering. Jesus was the Judge in stage one. Now, however, the judgment does not fall on the sinful and lost disciples, on sinful and lost Israel, or on sinful and lost humanity. "There is, in fact, a complete reversal, an exchange of roles" (p. 226). Judgment falls on him on whom it ought not to fall and not at all on those on whom it ought to fall. Again Barth makes explicit mention of the disciples, on whom (among others) the judgment should fall, but does not at all fall.

In Frei's exposition the third stage begins with Jesus' journey to Jerusalem and concludes with the ascension. This stage depicts "an individual and a series of events in connection with him that . . . are what they are in their own right" (p. 133). Jesus and his actions and the events befalling him are unsubstitutable, specific. As the passion narrative begins, the connection between Jesus and the kingdom of God becomes tenuous. Jesus is more and more the unsubstitutable character who will enact his own identity. The titles of the one who represents the kingdom are increasingly used with an ironic twist. The focus of the story, at this point, is on the unsubstitutable individual Jesus. What is remarkable in this final stage of the story is that the increasing action of God does not detract in the slightest from the increasingly sharp focus on Jesus' singularity. "Indeed, at the climactic point of the divine action, the resurrection, where God alone is active, it is Jesus alone who is manifest" (p. 135). In the resurrection appearance sequence, the singular, unsubstitutable Jesus, who has enacted his own identity, now identifies by his own unsubstitutable identity the meaning of the titles Son of Man, Lord, Christ. In the resurrection "he was most of all himself, and here most fully manifested as the individual, Jesus of Nazareth. . . . In focusing his identity, *i.e.,* who he is, the full sequence as such, passion, death and resurrection is one stage. Who is this man? He is Jesus of Nazareth, who, as this man and no other, is truly manifest as the Saviour, the presence of God" (pp. 136-37). The direction of the gospel story as a whole is unilinear — from no singularity to the fullest singularity.

What about "us" others? According to Frei's exposition the gospel story identifies Jesus of Nazareth as a specific individual in his own right who as such is manifested as the presence of God. And because he has specific identity, and because he has the specific identity he has (dying and rising for others he is manifested as the presence of God's action), we "others" have specific identity too (p. 138). This exposition is clear and helpful. Yet Frei does not mention the specific identity Jesus had for the disciples and, thus, for us, as the one who appointed, called, and sent them.[3]

For Barth, the third stage of the gospel story tells "of the forty days in which the same One whose history this was and had to be, was again in the midst of His disciples, differently, but still acting in time and space . . . beginning with them a new Gospel history, the time of His community . . . the time of the proclamation of this event. He Himself was and is this event, the origin and authority and power and object of the proclamation laid on the community" (p. 227). The narrative of the forty days is the proclamation of him who had been their Judge in Galilee and allowed himself to be judged in their place (and in that of all others) in Jerusalem and is now alive. The third stage gathers together all that has been told us in the earlier stages. Or, better, "it tells us how the sum which God Himself [in raising Jesus from the dead] . . . gathered together [of] all that had gone before [in Jesus' ministry and death] was revealed as such to the disciples . . . by Jesus Himself. . . . The Easter story is the record of how [the gospel story] became what it was . . . for the disciples, not by their own discovery, but by the act of God in the word and work of Jesus Himself" (p. 227).

The forty days are the climactic summation of all that Jesus had said and done and undergone and also of all that had been said and done and undergone by Israel as God's people. Moreover, Jesus in the forty days is the manifest Proclaimer of this fulfillment to his disciples and, as such, commissions them to proclaim what he made known to them in the forty days. Barth very nearly puts the emphasis of the Easter

---

3. I shall return later to what Frei says in *Identity,* chaps. 14ff.

story on Jesus' relationship with the apostles. It is at this point that his exposition is at a distance from Frei's, even while at other crucial points they are similar.

Even in their more general descriptions of the gospel story, then, Barth and Frei differ insofar as Barth gives great emphasis to Jesus' relationship with the twelve disciples whereas Frei scarcely mentions it. The difference becomes more sharply focused when Barth's exposition of the Gospels as descriptions of Jesus' appointment, calling, and sending of the apostles (still apropos of Jesus' identity) is set beside Frei's exposition of the Gospels as identity descriptions of Jesus by his application of an intention-action schema. The more specific comparison is necessary, for from it we will be in a position to see how attention to the gathering, upholding, and sending of the Twelve gives a clue for the interpretation of Scripture, which Barth makes available to us and Frei does not.[4]

## Differences in the Respective Expositions of the Three-Stage Gospel Story

### A Brief Outline

We will first give attention to the intention-action schema that Frei employs in asking about Jesus' identity.[5] To discover what a person is like we want to discover instances in which someone enacted a central intention. Ingredient in this issue of identity is the question of what circumstances befell a person and how he or she responded to them. "Identity is given in the mysterious coincidence of [a person's] intentional action with circumstances partly initiated by him, partly devolving upon him" (p. 94). What Jesus intended and enacted was perfect obedience to God; and "his obedience to God was one with his intention to do what had to be done on men's behalf" (p. 103). This is the beginning of the reply that Frei finds the gospel story gives to the question, "What is Jesus like?" However, what the gospel story describes is not intention alone, nor action alone, nor circumstance alone. Rather, Jesus

---

4. Is this simply a lacuna in Frei's work or does something take its place? At first, it is simply a lacuna, but then other statements of a wholly literary kind, helpful and proper in themselves, are used to fill it. What is ancillary is made primary.

5. *Identity,* chaps. 9, 10, and 11.

"becomes who he is in the coincidence of his enacted intention with the train of circumstances in which the story comes to a head" (p. 104).

Barth expands his brief account of the gospel story (*C.D.* IV/1, pp. 224-28) in an exposition of the three stages of the Gospels as the three stages of Jesus' choosing of his apostles (*C.D.* II/2, pp. 431-49). I shall now place this exposition beside Frei's exposition of the gospel story in terms of his intention-action schema.

In describing the three stages of the Gospel record, Barth speaks of the appointment, calling, and commissioning of the apostles. In his explication of the account of the appointment of the Twelve, Barth finds that what the appointment makes clear is that Jesus does not intend to be alone in the enactment of his mission. He appoints the disciples to participate actively in his work; he intends them to share actively in his work of proclamation. As he acts, his gathering of the apostles is ingredient in his acts. And his gathering of them has as its intention that they be "gatherers" with him. The choosing of the disciples belongs, then, to the enacted intention of Jesus, and thus to his identity.

Already in the Gospels and more prominently in the Acts of the Apostles we are presented with narratives about the enactment by the apostles of their intention in specific trains of circumstances. (In Acts we are given especially such a description of Paul, whom Barth numbers among the Twelve.) Barth makes clear (as does Frei) that there is no repetition of Jesus' identity in the apostle. Rather, even as Jesus' identity is enacted in the interaction between Jesus and God and in the interaction between Jesus and the apostles,[6] so the apostle's identity is enacted in terms of Jesus' action of appointing (gathering), calling (upholding), and sending (commissioning) the apostle and the apostle's action of learning from, receiving, and proclaiming Jesus — in sum, in enacting Jesus' intention for him.

While Frei helpfully demonstrates that Jesus cannot not be present — because it belongs to his identity to be present as Jesus of Nazareth — Barth finds it necessary to go further and say that it belongs to Jesus' identity to be present (a) as the One who specifically appointed, called, and sent the apostles and (b) as the Gatherer, Upholder, and Sender of those who come after the apostles by way of the apostles' learning from, reception of, and proclamation of Jesus. Hermeneutically

---

6. Jesus' interaction with Israel and, on the margin, with the Gentiles need not be the focus of our attention here.

this will mean that we will read the texts of the New Testament[7] in function of Jesus' gathering, upholding, and sending his first witnesses, and read subsequent exposition of Scripture in function of Jesus' gathering and upholding and sending subsequent hearers/witnesses by way of the witness of those he first gathered, upheld, and sent. Again, the New Testament is to be read in function of Jesus' enacted intention to gather, call, and send disciples; and subsequent exposition will be tested by its correspondence (in always fresh and surprising ways because in a new train of circumstances) to the learning from, reception of, and proclamation of Jesus by the first witnesses.

Now a certain procedural difficulty needs to be addressed in placing side by side Frei's intention-action schema and Barth's account of the appointment, calling, and commissioning of the apostles. Frei looks at the third stage of the gospel story (for him, the passion-death-resurrection sequence) in the employment of his intention-action schema, while Barth examines all three stages of the gospel story (for him, the Galilean ministry, the passion, the resurrection) in his exposition of the choosing of the apostles. The procedural difficulty is not insuperable, since for Barth the three stages not only overlap, but also the final stage — in which the commissioning occurs — includes and makes clear what was fully ingredient but hidden in the appointment and calling (pp. 431-32). So we may begin the comparison by recounting what Frei says about the intention-action of Jesus and then align with it what Barth says about the choosing of the apostles.

What was Jesus like? Frei enumerates three factors in the Gospel depiction of Jesus. First, he was obedient to God's will. Second, the manner of the enactment of his obedience entails the coexistence of power and powerlessness in his situation, but also the transition of one to the other. "It is his vicarious identification with the guilty and, at the climax of the story, his identification with the helplessness of the guilty that provide the Gospel's story of salvation" (p. 104). The pattern is at once simple and complex, for it is Jesus' helplessness that is his power to save others, and thus his power abides in his helplessness. Third, Jesus' enacted intention — to obey God's will and enact the good of humans on their behalf — meshes, in the story, with external circumstances. "His identity is revealed in the mysterious unity of his own decision and determination with the circumstances and events of his passion and death" (p. 105). "Circumstances" here bespeak neither

---

7. Also the Old Testament. This point will receive attention in due course.

chance nor fate, but rather cohere with the will of the Father, so that what happens is the interaction between Jesus and the one he calls "Father."[8]

Barth emphasizes the Great Commission of Matthew 28:18-20 in speaking about Jesus' commissioning of the disciples. "All power in heaven and earth has been given to me." Barth's attention is focused on the announcement of the identity of God's action with Jesus' appearance. Thus, Frei's third point about the interaction of the intention-action of Jesus with the intention-action of God and Barth's discussion of Jesus' transference of his mission to the apostles are fit for comparison.

In his first point Frei indicates that Jesus' identity is revealed in the enactment of his intention to be obedient to the mission to which God appointed him. The narratives that depict Jesus in the Garden of Gethsemane and on the cross are those which, Frei declares, tell us the most about Jesus' central intention to be obedient and about Jesus' central act of obedience. Here a degree of discrepancy in the procedure of my comparison between Frei and Barth should be acknowledged. For what I shall place side by side is Frei's account of Jesus' intended act of obedience and Barth's account of Jesus' appointment of the apostles. But only a *degree* of discrepancy need be acknowledged. Frei affirms that Jesus' obedience, while enacted fully on the cross and most tellingly revealed as his intention in the Garden of Gethsemane episode, requires the whole gospel story if his character as obedient to the Father is to be recognized. "His obedience exists solely as a counterpart to his being sent and has God for its indispensable point of reference. Jesus' very identity involves the will and purpose of the Father who sent him. He becomes who he is in the story by consenting to God's intention and by enacting [it]" (p. 107). From the outset, and therefore in what Barth regards as the first stage of the gospel story, there are references to Jesus being sent, and these appear not only in John but also in Luke (e.g., 4:43) and Matthew (e.g., 10:16). In sum, the very characteristic of Jesus' central intention, obedience, requires the context of the whole Gospel account, so that the enactment of his central intention can be clearly recognized to be obedience to the One who sent him. Jesus' obedience is his obedience to his mission. Barth's exposition of the references to

---

8. In comparing Barth and Frei we may observe that Barth's discussion of the calling of the apostles in terms of Jesus upholding them by his intercession for them corresponds to Frei's second point — to the pattern of Jesus' being powerful and powerless and to the pattern of his transition from the former to the latter.

Jesus' mission (his being sent) focuses on Jesus' relationship with those to whom he is (first) sent. Frei's discussion of "He Was Obedient" and Barth's discussion of Jesus' appointment of the apostles are, at least very nearly, apt for comparison.

## He Was Obedient

The gospel story, Frei observes, makes constant reference to Jesus' mission and his obedience to it (p. 106). This is a crucial point because it demonstrates that the center of Jesus' person is not within himself, but rather "in relation to the events of his life and the persons with whom he came in contact" (p. 107). Moreover, "His obedience exists solely as a counterpart to his being sent . . . [by God]. . . . Jesus' very identity involves the will and purpose of the Father who sent him. He becomes who he is in the story by consenting to God's intention and by enacting that intention in the midst of the circumstances that devolve around him as the fulfillment of God's purpose" (p. 107).

In the gospel story (1) Jesus is an unsubstitutable, specific individual who performs specific actions; (2) Jesus' identity is centered on his specific, obedient actions, which move to a certain goal; (3) Jesus has a self-focused identity. The patterns in the gospel story — of the coexistence of power and powerlessness and of the transition from power to powerless — which Frei discusses, are not conditions or qualities that exist apart from Jesus. These patterns are efficacious for salvation "because he holds them together in the enactment of his obedience to God" (p. 108). In sum, they describe Jesus' actions, or better, Jesus in his actions.

Frei's description of Jesus' intended action is two sided: (1) it is obedience to God; (2) it is saving of his fellow humans.

Barth's exposition of the texts about Jesus' appointment of the apostles gives the same clear attention, as does Frei, to the gospel story's constant reference to Jesus' mission and his obedience to it. And it is obvious that Barth no less than Frei sees that throughout the gospel story Jesus' obedience to his mission moves him inexorably toward his intercessory death. But ingredient in and necessary to this mission, throughout the gospel story, is Jesus' relationship with his disciples.[9] To Jesus' acknowledgment of and obedience to his mission in the first

---

9. Also his relation to Israel and to the nations, but that need not attract our attention here.

stage of the Gospels belongs his appointment of the apostles. ("Apostle" is the right word to use here, Barth indicates, since at their appointment Jesus promises to make them "fishers of men." Indeed, Barth uses "apostles" and "disciples" interchangeably and in this work the same interchangeability will be practiced.) Indeed, everything we find in this first stage of the gospel record is an elucidation of the apostles' appointment, according to Barth. Even as God, according to his will, sent Jesus, so Jesus intends to send apostles, and while the enactment of that intention waits on his intercession and exaltation, even in the first stage Jesus transfers to the Twelve the appointment and mission of Israel to the nations. He already intends that they shall actively participate in his mission.

Most important to the thesis I want to develop, Jesus' appointment of the Twelve to participate actively in his mission is ingredient in his activity and therefore in his identity. He came and comes to gather, uphold, and send, and this means (a) that his identity is that of Gatherer, Intercessor, and Commissioner of the apostles, and (b) that Jesus in that identity, therefore, gathers, calls, and sends men and women subsequent to the apostles by including them in his gathering, upholding, and sending of the Twelve.

Barth notes a number of points that elucidate the appointment of the apostles: Jesus "gathers" disciples that he may be accompanied by "gatherers." These gatherers do not "gather" independently of him, for they always depend wholly on him for their power. It is he who feeds the five thousand with the little the apostles have to offer. They are to deliver what he provides. His presence is required if the storm is not to overcome them, or if they are not to sink beneath the waves. In this first stage, the "gatherers with Him" ("the gatherers to be") are sent only to the lost sheep of the house of Israel, for Jesus has not yet traversed the path to the manifestation of his kingship over Israel and the nations. In this first stage the "gatherers to be" are to preach and also heal the sick and cast out demons. When they are constituted "effective gatherers" they shall still preach, but will baptize rather than heal the sick and cast out demons. The latter actions were to distinguish Jesus and his followers in the first stage of Jesus' mission from the prophets of the Old Testament. After Jesus' resurrection these signs are no longer required, although they are not prohibited.

The identity between Jesus and the apostles in this first stage is already intense. All the willing reception of their message is the reception of Jesus, and all the good shown them is shown to Jesus and is rewarded. "He who receives you, receives me." Everything said about the apostles' deeds and sufferings finds its meaning in the fact that they are Jesus' emissaries. This is why there is so little, really nothing, said of their achievements. The secret of their mission is that he is with them, and therefore they are able to be with him, not on their own behalf but on behalf of them to whom they are sent.

Frei indicates that Jesus obeyed God and enacted his neighbor's salvation. This was his enacted intention; in this is Jesus' identity. Frei says nothing to indicate that this enacted intention is other than effective; yet he does not explicate its effectiveness — its "strange" effectiveness. And this "effectiveness" belongs to Jesus' identity. He does not abstractly — that is, apart from his neighbor — enact his neighbor's good. In the first place (although this will be effective for lost and defecting Israel and for lost and defecting men and women of all nations) he appoints twelve pupils (stage 1), substitutes his back in place of theirs (stage 2), and is manifest to them in power (stage 3) so that they understand what they were taught, and understand that they were taught it for their neighbor's sake; and (anticipating what will be said below in respect of their call) so that they understand that his back received what was due them and their neighbors in such way that they and their neighbors need not receive what was their due. The Twelve (the eleven plus Paul, according to Barth's exposition) were appointed to learn this — and they did; they were called to receive his intercession — and they did. Or, Jesus appointed them to learn of him for their neighbor's sake and called them to receive his intercession for them as a promise for their neighbors. Their proclamation of him as Teacher, as Intercessor, and as King is the interaction of the enactment of his effective intention and the enactment (sufficient by his mercy) of their own intention (again sufficient by his mercy).

## Jesus' Power and Powerlessness

Frei begins his account of Jesus' power and powerlessness with the observation that the clearest indication of Jesus' intention is present in the final stage of the gospel story: "Yet not what I will, but what Thou wilt" (Mark 14:36). The transition from intention to enactment is depicted in the scene of Jesus' arrest, in which, according to Matthew (26:53-54), Jesus willingly relinquishes power. "Jesus affirms the will of God obediently by both initiating and consenting to the shape of events that now develop in their mysterious logic" (p. 110). Jesus intends to obey the will of God — to enact humans' good on their behalf — and the passion-crucifixion-resurrection sequence depicts its enactment. Jesus is identified in the enactment of his intention. The referent of Jesus' obedience is the will of God; the content of that obedience is the pattern of merciful, saving activity drawn from Deutero-Isaiah's depiction of the obedient, righteous servant. "It is the pattern of exchange" (p. 111). The pattern of exchange entails both the coexistence of power and powerlessness and the transition from one to the other. Even in the powerlessness of the crucifixion Jesus retains power; for example, Jesus' promise to the thief that he shall be with him in paradise (Luke 23:43), and the rulers' words — "He saved others, he cannot save himself." His power in his powerlessness also is indicated by his control over the events of his powerlessness: "I lay down my life . . . of my own accord" (John 10:16-17).

Yet there is also a genuine transition from power to powerlessness — for Jesus is genuinely helpless in this transition. In the story of the Garden of Gethsemane Jesus moves from liberty of action to the elimination of it by his own decision to consent to powerlessness and through the action of the authorities. "Once Jesus gives himself over to the authorities, his liberty of action will be at an end, and the result will be almost certain death for him" (p. 113). The point of transition is the Garden of Gethsemane. "Up to this point Jesus had had freedom and scope of movement. He had been portrayed as a figure of authority and power, but now in the Garden, with circumstances narrowed to the decisive point, it becomes part of his own free agency to enact the coincidence between his own decision and developing events. From that coincidence would develop the crucial pattern of events in which his identity would be enacted" (p. 114).

Frei describes the obedience of Jesus in terms of his holding together power and powerlessness (in their coexistence in the transition from the one to the other), but he does not develop the point with respect to Jesus' relationship with his disciples.

Barth's exposition of the second stage of the gospel story attends, as does Frei's, to Jesus as Intercessor. But Barth concentrates on Jesus' intercession as the action or enacted intention that upholds the disciples. According to Barth's exposition, the second stage of the gospel story runs from Jesus' turning from Galilee to Jerusalem, continues with his entry into Jerusalem, and concludes with his burial. On this road to death, Jesus calls his disciples to accompany him. The disciples are called to their function on this road to death, which is to attest Jesus' intercession. In their commissioning, in the third stage of the gospel story, they will be empowered to recognize this function.

Barth's exposition of the texts concerning Jesus' power and powerlessness, in this second stage, explores their interrelation with the texts concerning the apostles' power and powerlessness. Passages concerning the apostles' power are woven into the narrative depicting Jesus' road to death. We read: "on this rock I will build my church and the gates of hell will not prevail against it . . . I will give you the keys of the kingdom of heaven, and whatever you bind on earth shall be bound in heaven and whatever you loose on earth shall be loosed in heaven" (Matt. 16:18-19). But the depiction of the apostolate in this middle section of the Gospel account stands in stark contrast to Jesus' announcement of its power. (Indeed, four verses after Jesus' announcement of the apostles' power, he says to Peter, their representative who has fallen prey to temptation, "Get behind me Satan.") The depiction of the apostolate accompanying Jesus on his road to death "is one of absolute blindness in the face of the way Jesus has chosen for Himself," which he will and must follow to the end. It is one of absolute misunderstanding about the way to follow him, about the apostles' capacity to follow him, and about what they may hope in following him. It is, in sum, a depiction of their denial of him (p. 439).

Does not their denial seem to indicate a revocation of their appointment in the first stage? Barth finds that the Gospels make the opposite case. The activity dominating this period is Jesus' death on the cross. He must suffer it alone. He alone is Intercessor. And he intercedes in the first place for these deniers. The event of Jesus' death on the cross is the mystery of their calling. While Jesus' disciples abandon him, he does not abandon them. He upholds them throughout this period not only by warnings and commands, but also by assurances and promises that his intercession and exaltation make good. The institution of the Lord's Supper during this period is the strongest possible affirmation of their calling.

In giving an account of the power and powerlessness of the apostles, as it is depicted in the second stage of the Gospel narrative, Barth pays particular attention to Matthew 16. "We ought never explain the 'You are Peter' independently, separating it from . . . its relationship to the second part of the Gospel account, which culminates in the passion story" (p. 440). Peter is the spokesman of the Twelve. "If we want to make a 'prince of the apostles' out of this spokesman," then in view of what we are told in this middle section we must say that "he is this only as their leader . . . in defection" (p. 441). This is what Peter is apart from Jesus. And yet Peter's confession is the foundation and invincibility of the church. Because Jesus put his back in place of Peter's, because his death canceled the power and effect of Peter's denial, only Peter's appointment remains and is confirmed and purified. Indeed, calling is the confirmation and purification of the disciples in their appointment.

The apostle subsequently is commissioned to proclaim Jesus to people of all nations, but the commissioned apostle had first been called. Thus, only as one called does the apostle proclaim Jesus. This means that only as one who is himself upheld by Jesus does the apostle proclaim Jesus — even as he (the apostle) calls others to receive this upholding. When Peter and the apostolate (and through the apostolate the whole community) loose and remit sins, it is as defectors and deniers, who are — despite their defection and denial — upheld by Christ's intercession. Being upheld by Christ is their calling, and their confession is their recognition of their calling. In sum, the apostle proclaims Christ, and does so as one called, which means as one who acknowledges his defection (powerlessness) and recognizes his own and all others' reconciliation — despite his own and all others' defection — in the cancellation of the power and effect of all human defection by Christ's intercession. When the apostle fails to recognize his calling (his purification by Christ and his need for it), that is, when he fails to acknowledge Christ's power and his need for it in every moment, his proclamation is powerless. Contrariwise, when he recognizes Christ's liberation of him from this powerlessness, he is able to proclaim this liberation with power to (as true for) all who hear him.

Barth refers to the whole middle section of the gospel story, which is dominated by the account of Jesus' intercessory death, as the period of the calling of the disciples. Subsequently the disciples will become the commissioned proclaimers of Jesus — but as those who are called. In no sense, in relation to sin, do they stand in their own power. By Jesus' intercession they stand, and as they proclaim him as the Intercessor for their own sins and for those of all their hearers, they are the rock, the guarantee of the church.

Frei's exposition of the narrative about Jesus' intercession, its observation of the pattern of the coexistence of power and powerlessness and the pattern of the transition of one to the other, is, in several of its features, as penetrating as Barth's exposition and even attends more closely to some literary features than does Barth's.[10] But Frei

---

10. I refer here to Frei's attention to the change in circumstances to which Jesus consents and which he initiates.

leaves altogether out of his account the effect of the exchange on the apostles, whereas Barth denominates it as calling and executes his exposition in terms of that heading.

Barth observes that the apostles themselves are powerless; Jesus' relinquishment of power, his transition to powerlessness, is the foundation of the invincible power given the apostles — the power to loose and to bind people from and to their sins, the power of entrance into the kingdom of heaven. (Attention to Frei's terminology may be helpful here in exposing Barth's explication.) In relinquishing power, Jesus still retained power. ("He saved others, he cannot save himself.") The apostles themselves, in a fashion that reverses Jesus' pattern, are powerless. That is the point Barth stresses in his exposition of the middle section of the Gospels. And on their own they never become powerful. Their deaths will not bring the forgiveness of sins, they have no power of themselves to bring life from the dead, nor does their teaching bring life except that they deliver what Jesus teaches them. The power of Jesus' powerlessness (his death) is what upholds them and their proclamation, for his powerlessness is his intercession for them made eternal in his resurrection from the dead. Jesus does not merely appoint the apostles, although so saying does not diminish their appointment. They are appointed to share in his work as revealers (although none of them is appointed to be intercessor or redeemer). But the apostles have no power to be revealers, except that Jesus does not merely appoint his apostles to receive and to share his mission as Revealer, but also upholds them at every point of their mission. He upholds them at every point by his intercessory death.

To guard against a Gnostic interpretation of the second stage of the Gospel account, it is of first-order importance to observe that the New Testament depicts the Savior as a specific individual. And Frei does this exceedingly well. But ingredient in this depiction is the fact that this specific Savior gathered, upheld, and sent specific individuals. Jesus' identity as Gatherer, Upholder, and Sender is his identity as the Gatherer, Upholder, and Sender of these specific twelve men. His identity as Gather, Upholder, and Sender of these twelve means he ever gathers, upholds, and sends men and women by way of these unsubstitutable men, his apostles, and this activity can no more be described in a mythological or Gnostic fashion than can Jesus himself be so described.

In prospect of some thinking about the hermeneutical implications of this section, I proffer a three-sentence summary of Barth's exposition (although in Frei's terminology!): The mission of the apostle requires the intercession of Christ at every point. Without Christ's intercession it is powerless. But Christ's intercession is his powerlessness; thus, Christ's powerlessness is the apostle's power — or, more fully, the powerlessness of the apostle is made powerful (only) by the power of Christ's powerlessness. How this observation affects the interpretation of the New Testament will have to await a later discussion. For the moment I may simply indicate that what the apostles said, they said in the power of Jesus' intercession for them, themselves testifying to their powerlessness apart from this intercession of Jesus.

While Jesus' intercession is "once and *for all*" and finally is the calling of all — that is, is that act by which all are upheld — it is, with respect to revelation, the calling of the Twelve — that is, the act by which they, in their participation in Jesus' mission, are upheld.

### *Jesus and God*

In describing the intention-action of Jesus, Frei spoke of how it entailed Jesus' giving up power and yet how power and powerlessness coexisted in him. Frei turns next to the description of the interaction of the intention-action of Jesus with the intention-action of God.

When Jesus relinquishes power, to whom does the power to initiate action pass? To his accusers and judges and to those whom they represent. In sum, to "historical forces." But "there is a mysterious and fascinating coincidence or 'mergence' between divine action and the 'historical forces' at their common point of impact — Jesus' judgment and death" (p. 116). Indeed, according to John, "at their common point of impact" Pilate's power and God's power cohere (John 19:10-11). The rising initiative of the "historical forces" and of God both seem to increase in proportion to the decrease of Jesus' initiative. This matter is complex, however, since in this same sequence of the third stage of the gospel story Jesus' intention and action become increasingly identified with those of God, whose initiative coheres with the "historical forces," even while the distinction of Jesus' agency and that of God remains (cf. Mark 15:34, the cry of dereliction). In the sequence, God supersedes Jesus; yet Jesus retains his identity, even though the intention-action of God and the intention-action of Jesus are increasingly identified. "On the cross the intention and action of Jesus are fully superseded by God's, and what emerges is a motif of supplantation and yet identification" (p. 118). This is not subordination of Jesus to God for, then, Jesus would have no identity of his own. "Instead, we see in the story a crucified human saviour, who is obedient to God's intention and to his action" (p. 118). Paul describes this as Jesus obediently making God's intention and action his own (Phil. 2:6-11).

In the Synoptic Gospels (upon which Frei concentrates his attention), the dominance of God's activity over that of Jesus reaches its apex in the account of Jesus' resurrection. In the resurrection God and God alone is active. Jesus was active in his ministry; during his passion he becomes increasingly passive; finally he cannot act at all — he is dead and buried. In the resurrection *God and God alone acts* — but *only Jesus appears*, the same Jesus who enacted his intention in a preliminary way in his ministry and in a final way in his passion. In the resurrection narratives God, whose initiative has supplanted that of Jesus, is scarcely in evidence and the word "God" is hardly mentioned. "It is *Jesus and Jesus alone who appears* just at this point, when God's supplantation of him is complete. . . . In his passion and death the initiative of Jesus disappears more and more into that of God, but in the resurrection, where the initiative of God is finally and decisively climaxed and he alone is and can be active, the sole identity to mark the presence of that activity is Jesus. . . . Jesus of Nazareth, he and none other, marks the presence of the action of God" (p. 121).

In the story Jesus is not simply in need of redemption but is redeemed. "The resurrection is the vindication in act of his own intention and God's. . . . In the unity and transition between his need of redemption and his being in fact redeemed, Jesus' identity is focused, and the complex relation and distinction between his identity and that of God is manifested" (p. 121). Frei notes that an oddity has cropped up in his use of terms. He has indicated that "Jesus is set forth in his resurrection as the manifestation of the action of God" (p. 124). This is an oddity since the correlate of *action* is "enactment in public occurrence" and the correlate of *manifestation* is *self*. God's act of raising Jesus from the dead is an act in which Jesus' identity is *manifested*, rather than being achieved in public occurrence. Yet this manifestation of Jesus' identity in his resurrection is an enacted event, according to the sermon in Acts (10:40). This oddity, a combination of self-manifestation and intention-action, belongs to the complex pattern of the relation of Jesus' actions and God's actions depicted in the gospel story.

Frei earlier had made clear why Jesus' identity cannot be described apart from speaking of God: A description of Jesus' enacted intention is a description of his central intention to enact the will of

God. Now Frei has provided a second reason why Jesus' identity cannot be described apart from speaking of God: In Jesus' resurrection from the dead, he is manifested as the presence of God's action, and thus Jesus of Nazareth is the manifestation of God's enacted intention.

Barth's exposition of the resurrection narratives, despite its concentration upon the Great Commission, is, at critical points, in concurrence with Frei's commentary.[11] First, "in this time the *man* Jesus was manifested among [the disciples] in the mode of *God*" (*C.D.* III/2, p. 448, italics added). Second, like Frei, Barth emphasizes that the Jesus who was raised is, according to the Gospel account, the Jesus of Nazareth whom the disciples accompanied in Galilee and to and in Jerusalem. "To be an apostle of Jesus Christ means not only [in the forty days] to have seen Him with one's eyes and to have heard Him with one's ears, but to have touched Him physically. . . . Unless Christ's resurrection was a resurrection of the body, we have no guarantee that it was the decisively acting Subject Jesus Himself, the *man* Jesus who rose from the dead" (p. 448). But Barth gives a different emphasis than does Frei to the fact that in the forty days the man Jesus was *manifested in the mode of God.* For we must give attention to every part of the statement that the man Jesus was *manifested in the mode of God to the disciples.* Frei gives virtually no stress to *to the disciples.* Barth observes that the man Jesus' manifestation *in the mode of God* has ingredient in it effective power; that is, effective power belongs to Jesus' manifestation in the mode of God and is a demonstration of it. In this manifestation Jesus exercises this power by confirming his appointment and calling of the disciples in his commissioning of them not with mere power but with almighty power (Matt. 28:18). Note that Barth is not saying that Jesus' power in the forty days proves his resurrection (which for him is a foolish construal of the text), but rather that the risen Jesus demonstrates the power of his exaltation (which is the power to reveal the cancellation of sin accomplished in his death and therein to confirm the calling of the disciples, and is, also, the power to reveal that what he accomplished was the will of the Father and therein to confirm his mission and thus the appointment of the disciples) by his commissioning of the disciples. In sum, Jesus demonstrates his being in the mode of God by, in his declarations, overcoming the fears, griefs, bewilderment, doubts, and disbeliefs of his disciples. His commissioning of them indicates that their participation in his mission will neither depend on their resources or achievements nor be

---

11. The next several page references are to *C.D.* III/2.

thwarted by their inadequacy or even by any obstacles that they might put in its way (p. 449).

To gather how central Jesus' relationship with the disciples is in the narratives about Jesus' resurrection, according to Barth's explication of them, it is worth quoting him at length:

> If the prologues of the two books [of Luke] . . . are read in light of the Emmaus story we shall see how the various elements are interconnected . . . : the history of the words and works of Jesus, then, as a link in the chain, the history of . . . the forty days; and finally the history of the apostles. [Luke] does not allow the first history . . . to sink into the mere past in the final history to which [Luke] himself belongs. For the latter would be nothing without the former; it is simply its sequel. And the intervening history of the Easter period is . . . a revelation of the first history which dispels the errors, prejudices and blindness of the apostles. . . . Hence, the New Testament necessarily took the form of "the Gospel and the apostle." (Pp. 472-73)

It was the Jesus of the Galilean ministry and of the Jerusalem passion, both of which the disciples witnessed, who came again among the disciples in the forty days "emerging from the past as a figure of the present, alive for evermore, abiding with them as Lord" (p. 473). The apostle executes his appointment and calling, in the power of his commissioning, by declaring that the Teacher Jesus of yesterday who is one and the same as the Intercessor Jesus of yesterday is alive today by virtue of Who he is, as manifested in his resurrection from the dead.

Both Frei and Barth stress that the man Jesus of Nazareth was raised from the dead. Both emphasize that his resurrection is his manifestation as the presence of God. But Barth emphasizes that this manifestation of Jesus in the mode of God during the forty days was to the disciples. Indeed, his manifestation in the mode of God is demonstrated by the power Jesus exercises in his relationship with the disciples during the forty days. Frei leaves the point wholly undeveloped.

So far I have presented Barth's more general comments about the Easter narratives. Attention to his more detailed commentary on the descriptions of the commissioning of the apostles that occur in these narratives makes even clearer his emphases.[12] Matthew places the commissioning in Galilee, thus closing the circle of Jesus' activity and that

---

12. The following page references are to *C.D.* II/2.

which is ingredient in it — the founding of the apostolate. Luke places it in Jerusalem from which, following Pentecost, the apostles are sent to the nations. Despite this difference Barth finds a common content in the two accounts and lists several elements of it.

First, in Luke, when Jesus appeared to the disciples, they were confused and frightened (24:37); in Matthew "some doubted" (28:17). Of themselves, they still "are not in any sense suitable instruments for the carrying-out of their appointment. The person of Jesus Himself was still necessary to create for them the relationship to Him which enabled them, as sent by Him, to perform what He performed" (p. 433).

Second, according to Matthew Jesus begins his commission to the disciples with the words, "All power is given to me in heaven and on earth" (28:18). The disciples are commanded to share in this power. This finds a parallel in Luke's depiction where Jesus is *the* expositor of Scripture (24:13-35). Who could be such other than the One who is the bearer of God's power? Where Matthew gives an account of Jesus' command that the disciples share his almighty power, Luke gives an account of Jesus uncovering all of Scripture to the disciples by revealing himself as its content. This has a twofold effect upon the disciples. It constitutes them the witnesses to Jesus as the Fulfiller of Scripture and to Jesus as *the* Proclaimer of Scripture.

Third, in Matthew's account Jesus commissions the disciples to make men and women of all nations "my disciples." This is a confirmation of Jesus' appointment of the disciples, but the Teacher/pupil relationship is now deepened by the relationship of King/subject. And the Teacher/pupil relationship is also broadened, for Jesus by way of his first pupils is now the Teacher of all men and women. In Luke's account Jesus, expositing Scripture to his disciples in terms of its expectation of his death and resurrection, directs them to preach in his name to all nations the turning accomplished in him for the forgiveness of sins (24:47). In Luke, the content of the proclamation, Jesus' intercession for sinners, is made explicit. Yet this does not distance it from Matthew's account. This is the case, first, because this proclamation of the forgiveness of sins cannot be separated from the proclamation of his name. The proclamation of the disciples, according to both Matthew and Luke, will be a summons to faith in Christ. This is the case, second, because Matthew does not neglect the content that is explicit in Luke's account, namely Jesus' intercession for sinners. The disciples are commanded to baptize, to perform the act which is the sign of Jesus' effective intercession for sinners.

Finally, in both Matthew's and Luke's accounts the commission given to the disciples is directly connected with the promise of Jesus' presence. We read in Matthew 28:20b, "Lo I am with you always, even to the end of the world." He who has almighty power is with them in their mission; this binds their mission, and themselves as his emissaries, to him. He will always confess them as they confess him before men (Matthew 10). We read in Luke 24:49, "I send the promise of my Father upon you; but remain in the city, until you are clothed with power from on high." This promise of the Holy Spirit, fulfilled at Pentecost, is the promise that "the apostles are what they are and have what they have because and as Jesus wills that it should be so and fashions them accordingly, constituting Himself the substance of their commission, the power for its execution, . . . [and] its criterion" (p. 435).

Frei emphasizes that Jesus intended to obey God's will that he enact the good of men and women on their behalf. And he enacted this intention. Further, in his resurrection Jesus is manifested as the enacted intention of God. There is no ground upon which to distinguish Barth from Frei on these points. Even Barth's emphasis on the active agency of Jesus during the forty days, that is, on Jesus' act of commissioning the disciples, does not necessarily distance him from Frei's exposition. Only Barth's emphasis on the content of that agency, Jesus' relationship with the disciples, compels comment on their difference in exposition.

Certainly Frei says that in the resurrection narrative the identity of Jesus is focused such that from its depiction of Jesus the earlier narratives in the Gospels are to be explicated. But Barth explains the point. In the first stage of the gospel story Jesus, the Teacher, appoints the apostles; in the second stage Jesus, the Intercessor, calls, that is, upholds, the apostles; in the third stage Jesus, manifested in the mode of God, commissions with power the apostles: They are to teach what the Teacher of all men and women taught them (and teaches now by way of the apostles' teaching) and they are to proclaim that he by whom the forgiveness of their sins was accomplished accomplishes the forgiveness of sins for all flesh (and reveals this by way of the apostles' preaching and baptizing).

Frei carefully explicates the relationship between Jesus and God depicted in the texts of the New Testament and indicates how — in this relationship — Jesus' identity is rendered. Barth carefully explicates the relationship between Jesus and the apostles depicted in the texts of the New Testament and indicates how — in this relationship — Jesus' identity is rendered. (Barth also observes in the gospel story the beginning of the identity description of the apostles. But that identity description only begins in the Gospels and requires the second part of the New Testament canon for its full rendering.) Barth does not neglect Frei's point, but Frei does neglect Barth's point. Barth observes how the two emphases — Jesus' relationship with God, and Jesus' relationship with the apostles — are held together in the New Testament. Jesus, a man manifested in the mode of God during the forty days, is the Royal Man. He exercises the power of God, and this is *indicated* by his commissioning of the apostles, *depicted* in the Gospels, and *demonstrated* — in the account given by the second part of the New Testament canon — by the proclamation of the apostles.

## Summary

Jesus appointed disciples to learn from and finally of him. He not only intended to appoint them, but effectively appointed them, although this "effectively" awaited his manifestation in the mode of God during which he commissioned them. This "effectively" bespeaks power. (And this power is concretely demonstrated in public enactment — there is nothing here of the power of the inner self, celebrated by ancient and modern mythology.) But power is not a simple concept in the gospel story. Jesus holds together power and powerlessness and relinquishes power for powerlessness. In the first place the relinquishment of power is enacted (in obedience to God) for the disciples. In giving up power, Jesus intercedes for the blind, weak, denying apostles. Their powerlessness is not finally an obstacle to the Gospel, but rather the instrument for the manifestation of the power of Christ's powerlessness. Christ upholds the disciples, making their powerlessness a vehicle of power. Not any power, of course, but the power of salvation. This power needs to be manifested first to the disciples and finally to all flesh. Jesus' appearances in the forty days is the manifestation of this power to the disciples. And that this manifestation is on the way to all flesh is attested in the record of the apostles' proclamation (or mission) in the second half of the New Testament canon.

Frei has demonstrated that modern biblical interpretation has been an "eclipse of biblical narrative." That narrative often has been fitted into a "mythological mode of interpretation" and at other times fitted to a "historical mode of interpretation," dependent upon a contemporary view of "what is history." Frei advocates an explicative reading of the biblical text, and represents such a reading in his work of New Testament exposition. It is only that he concentrates his attention on the relationship between Jesus and God and, more briefly, on the relationship between Jesus and Israel and on the relationship between Jesus and the kingdom, and only as an addendum on Jesus and the church. One does not find in his work an attention to the relationship of Jesus with the disciples, and this is most surprising since that relation forms a crucial hermeneutical basis for the explication of the New Testament and, therefore, for Scripture as a whole.[13]

Why does the relationship of Jesus with the apostles form a crucial hermeneutical basis for the explication of the New Testament? In tendering a preliminary reply to this question reference may be made to Barth's exposition. The first stage of the gospel story has as a major integrating theme the appointment of the apostles. If the major theme is the coming of Jesus, a strong subsidiary theme is his appointment of those to whom he first came, who are to witness to his coming and to be the vehicle of all people's knowledge of his coming. If the major theme of the second stage of the gospel story is the intercessory death of Christ, a strong subsidiary theme — made evident by the account of the Last Supper — is the calling of those who, themselves upheld by his intercession (of which they so totally are in need), are to proclaim the Lord's death until he comes. If the major theme of the third stage of the gospel story is the manifestation of the man Jesus — in his self-focused identity — in the mode of God, ingredient in this manifestation are those to whom he is so manifest. Indeed, the power of this manifestation, or the presence of the Royal Man in power, is explicitly promised to *their* mission, and to their persons in their mission. And the fulfillment of this promise is depicted in the Acts of the Apostles and attested in the New Testament Epistles and Apocalypse. Regarding the three stages of the gospel story in their overlapping unity, we may say that the text depicts Jesus as effectively gathering, upholding, and sending the apostles. He is the Gatherer, Upholder, and Sender; the disciples are the gathered, upheld, and sent by whom many (or all) are gathered, upheld, and sent.

Two hermeneutical bases for the explication of the New Testament are indicated. First, we will read the New Testament texts as exponents of the event of the gathering, upholding, and commissioning of the apostles, which is ingredient in the event of Christ's coming,

---

13. I say "surprising" since the subtitle of Frei's work of exposition is "The Hermeneutical Bases of Dogmatic Theology."

intercession, and revealing enthronement. (And the Old Testament texts will be read as exponents of the event of Israel's being gathered, upheld, and even provisionally commissioned by him whom it expected.) Second, we will understand the church subsequent to the apostolate to be the event of being gathered, upheld, and sent by Jesus as it is included in the gathering, upholding, and sending of the first apostles.

What are the consequences of saying this for the reading of the New Testament? First, every New Testament text (and finally every Old Testament text) will be explicated in terms of its occurrence or eventuation in the gathering, upholding, and sending of the disciples by Jesus. Second, every New Testament text (and finally every Old Testament text) will be applied to the present situation of the church (and to its relation to those beyond the church) in terms of the church's inclusion in the gathering, upholding, and sending of the disciples by Jesus. The applicative sense, in this way, is not so much merely controlled by the explicative sense but ingredient in it.

# 2 *The Indefiniteness of Myth and the Definiteness of the Gospel*

Mythological readings of New Testament texts are often enough attempted. That is, one reads the gospel story of salvation and comes to a deeper understanding of the self, and this deeper understanding is salvation. But the gospel story itself does not support such a reading of it. Frei remarks that unsubstitutable identity is not the stuff of myth. In the Gospels Jesus is depicted as a specific, self-focused, unsubstitutable person. In demonstrating that the Gospels are "identity descriptions" of the specific Savior, the man Jesus of Nazareth, Frei demonstrates what places them outside the category of myth. In so doing he provides the fundamental point in distinguishing the Gospels from myth. However, in attending to Barth's exposition of the Gospels, we found that, in making clear the *specific* identity of Jesus, the Gospels make equally clear that the relationship of Jesus to others is *specific*. Frei, while not wholly neglecting this point, leaves it undeveloped. The Gospels and indeed the whole New Testament, according to Barth's exposition, do not lead us to the affirmation that the specific man Jesus is related in an indefinite way to all others as their Savior. Rather, Jesus appoints, calls, and commissions specific men (the Twelve) and gathers, upholds, and sends many or all others by way of the specific appointment, calling, and commissioning of the Twelve.[1]

1. Is this, then, an endorsement of the rubric, "Outside the church there is no salvation"? By posing this question and searching Barth's exposition for his answer to it, we can focus our attention upon his account of (the specificity of) Jesus' relationship with the disciples and, by way of them, others.

Jesus appoints, calls, and commissions the Twelve for the sake of every man

Frei's account of "the saviour myth" and his rejection of it as a description of the gospel story occur in chapter six of *Identity*. While attending to what he says about how "the saviour myth" fails to correspond to the description of the Savior of the gospel story, I will add some preliminary comments about how "the saviour myth" also fails to correspond to the gospel story's description of the Savior's relationship with his disciples. These comments, in accord with what Frei says but developing what he does not, will then be amplified by an examination of Barth's expository discussion of the implications of Jesus' gathering, upholding, and sending of the Twelve for his relationship with all those who come after the Twelve.

## Myth and Gospel

Although "the myth of salvation" is a phrase that could be used to represent a nature religion, in which the cycle or rhythm of life binds the human and organic nature together, Frei, while noting the point, concentrates his attention on "the myth of salvation" as it appears in a variety of Gnostic forms. Frei thinks of Gnosticism as no less modern

---

and woman. The news of the apostles' passive inclusion in his intercession and exaltation and of their active participation in his mission is news that the apostles are to bear to the ends of the earth. Not for their own glory are they to bear this news, but as the announcement of the inclusion of all others with them in Christ's intercession and exaltation and of the prospective participation of all others with them in their share in Christ's mission. Barth takes care to say that the apostles do not effect this inclusion and participation, but announce it. The force of this is that all are objectively included and participant in Christ's work and person. So the specificity of Jesus' relationship with all others objectively is that all are included in Jesus' appointment, calling, and sending of the Twelve. This is the specific shape the salvation of all takes. Subjectively salvation is the acknowledgment, recognition, and confession of this appointment, calling, and sending in public act, such an acknowledgment as the apostles made. Barth's exposition indicates that while this specific shape of salvation, objectively and subjectively, is to be affirmed against mythological (or Gnostic) generalities, yet it is not the Christian's task to prescribe, that is, to decide, who is saved and who is not. Salvation is objectively Jesus' appointment, calling, and commissioning of his disciple and subjectively is a man's or woman's public act of acknowledging these. But what constitutes a genuine acknowledgment is determined by God's decision and intention and not by the Christian or even by the church. (While Barth takes notice of the power given to the apostolate to bind and to loose people from their sins, announced in Matthew 16, he refers this power to the Word the apostles preach and not to their personal inclinations and perspectives.)

than ancient. His account of it is as follows: Myth, for the Gnostic, is a story form employed to evoke a kind of interior insight.[2] Human life in nature and society exists in alienation from its essential being. The myth of a dying and rising savior invokes an awareness of how human identity — disrupted in living at the surface level of life — is regained through a perception of this disruption at the surface of life and of a deeper self beneath it. This perception arises from "a shock of recognition" so profound that it can be evoked only by symbolical expression, not by explanatory discourse. That is, there is an ineffable unity of the alienated self (at the surface) with the true self (in the depths) which, being profound, can only find expression and awareness in myth, one of which forms is the myth of the dying and rising savior. The savior is at once divine but also archetypal human, since in the figure there are present the qualities of falling and returning — and the strange unity of both movements — which are the qualities present in all who gain this awareness of the true state of things.

Is the dying and rising savior myth like the gospel story? Frei describes four contrasts and finally speaks of the real difference between the mythological story and the gospel story. (1) The Gnostic redeemer has to be redeemed from his own alienation. Representative of all humans, he himself is alienated. "The redeemer in [the Gospel story] . . . incurs no guilt of his own from which he would have to be redeemed, although indeed he must be saved from death and evil . . . [which] . . . guilty men [and demonic powers] inflict upon him" (p. 57). (2) Christ's need for redemption (of this latter sort) appears much greater than that of the Gnostic savior, his powerlessness more drastic and complete. (3) In the gospel story Christ's need of redemption (his powerlessness) and his death have saving efficacy, but not as a stage in a rhythm of dying and rising. Each event in the story — passion, death, resurrection — has an integrity; none belongs to a process (e.g., of the human psyche) or to a pattern of history. (4) In the gospel story Jesus saves others through the coincidence of his powerlessness with his obedience. He puts his innocent back in the place of others' guilty backs, becoming powerless for them. The Gnostic savior saves the alienated by being himself alienated, indicating therein the organic unity of alienation and innocence.

The real difference between the dying and rising savior myth

2. *Mythos* is the Greek word for story. Frei uses the word "myth" as a genre indicator.

and the gospel story is the latter's identification of the Savior as a specific, unsubstitutable person: Jesus of Nazareth. No other human can substitute for Jesus. Moreover, in the gospel story, Jesus largely identifies the savior figure rather than the reverse. The Gnostic myth does not identify the savior in the story with a specific, individual human being. Those who reach awareness through the myth come to recognize in the savior figure in whom innocence, alienation, and redemption flow together "their presence to themselves" (p. 60). All this, as myth, takes place out of time — this unity of humans and savior, and, indeed, this unity of fall and redemption. This latter unity of opposites (fall and redemption) means "that one's identity and the acceptance of [one's] non-identity are one" (p. 61). There is no self-focused identity in this. "This insight into ourselves — into the common non-entity of our [own] presence and identity — is what the 'rising' of the saviour comes to mean in the Gnostic saviour accounts" (p. 61). This is in contrast to the gospel story, in which Jesus, in his self-focused identity, "determines the story as the crucial person in the story" (p. 62).

According to Frei, the anti-Gnostic character of the gospel story is demonstrated by the unsubstitutable character of the human Savior. But more attention than Frei gives it must also be accorded to the specific character of Jesus' relationship with his disciples. Taking into account Frei's points, but now in reverse order, the following comments can be and need to be made about the anti-Gnostic account in the gospel story of Jesus' relationship with his disciples: (4) The relation between the savior and the saved in Gnostic myth is one of solidarity in alienation. Jesus' relationship with his apostles in the gospel story is not founded in a commonality of sin, but rather in the intercession of Jesus in his innocence for their guilt. "This is my body broken for you. This is my blood shed for you." In Barth's terms, Jesus *calls* or *upholds* the apostles. (3) The Gnostic myth bespeaks a unity of the depicted savior with the saved founded in a common organic rhythm of dying and rising — a rhythm reflected in the human psyche and, perhaps, in macrocosmic humanity. But Jesus' relationship with the disciples follows no such organic process or pattern. Jesus appoints, calls, and commissions them. Each event has a uniqueness or an integrity. "The bond between events in the Gospel story simply has no meaning and does not exist apart from the occurrence of the events themselves in their sequence within the story" (p. 57). Each event is irreducibly unique. (2) In Gnostic myth there is a way through alienation inherent in alienation itself. Contrariwise, in the gospel story Jesus stood utterly in need of the act of the One who sent him. The parallel in Jesus' relationship with the disciples is that there is no way to Jesus open to the disciples. They do not "discover" him according to their capacity or incapacity, or according to their self-realization, or even according to their skill as biblical interpreters. In commissioning them, the man Jesus in the mode of God removes from them their blindness, prejudices, and errors. (1) In Gnostic myth the savior is alienated. In the gospel story Jesus in his ministry, while within the circle of his disciples, the multitudes, and the rulers of the people, speaks and acts in such a way that his being and thinking and willing are in antithesis to the whole being and thinking and willing of all of these people. According to Barth's exposition, this is what constitutes him their Judge and Teacher. Jesus in this sense is inaccessible to all of these people, including the disciples. Yet he gathers the disciples in their antithetical being, willing, and thinking into the kingdom, separating them from their antipathy to the kingdom by his intercession and by sharing his kingly power with them in his exaltation. While his righteousness in the first place makes him inaccessible to sinful and lost men and women, including the disciples, his righteousness in the second place, by making the disciples righteous, makes him accessible to the disciples — and to all others by way of their confession and proclamation of being made righteous.[3]

What distinguishes Jesus' relationship with the disciples as depicted in the gospel story from the relation of savior and saved in Gnostic myth is that Jesus' appointment, calling, and commissioning of the apostles are public enactments, not primarily occurrences in the inner world of the self. Jesus' calling of the apostles consists in the warnings and commands, promises and assurances he gives them, which he makes good by suffering a public execution for them. His commissioning of them has as a demonstration of its power their public testimony going to the ends of the earth. And his appointment of them has its public demonstration in the existence of the apostolate and also in the existence of the Christian community following upon it in replication of it (although the replication is always replication with respect to new circumstances).

To indicate the real difference between Gnostic myth and the gospel story, Frei demonstrates that the Savior in the gospel story is

---

3. Not that the apostles proclaim their own righteousness, but that they are made righteous by Christ's call (intercession) and know it by way of Christ's commissioning of them (in his exaltation).

a specific, unsubstitutable person. The specific man Jesus identifies the title "Savior." Frei's constructive and careful work, however, is insufficient if we are to speak of Christ's presence to others in a way that corresponds to the gospel story (and, at this point too, to keep a distance from Gnostic myth), and if we are to explicate biblical texts in terms of what they tell us about Christ's presence to others, and to resist "mythologizing" Christ's presence — along with his identity. A greater sufficiency in the discussion of Christ's presence and for the explication of New Testament texts can occur if we take into account the gospel story's depiction of (the unsubstitutable man) Jesus identifying, in specific public actions, who his apostles are (indicating his relationship with them): His apostles are the ones he appointed, called, and sent in the specific way in which he appointed, called, and sent them. He was accessible to men — these men — in this way. And all others are given access to him by way of their being included in this sphere of Jesus-appointed accessibility. No follower of Jesus can fashion the character and timing of his or her relationship with Jesus. Just as the Twelve received all that they received and were all that they were by way of Jesus' specific, public activity with them, so is this true of all others, only now by way of what the apostles had and were. In sum, all others, who are disciples after the Twelve, are such as ones who were and are appointed, called, and commissioned by Jesus by his inclusion of them (in their circumstances) in the appointment, calling, and commissioning of the Twelve, as that is specifically depicted in the gospel story. Indeed, the whole church is gathered, upheld, and sent as it is included by Jesus in his gathering, upholding, and sending of the Twelve. The relationship of Jesus with his followers is as specific as Jesus' own identity.

## Barth on the Specific Character of Jesus' Relationship with His Apostles

We have already looked at Barth's exposition of Gospel texts concerning Jesus' appointment, calling, and commissioning of the Twelve. As we saw, Barth does not think that the New Testament texts suggest that Jesus' appointment, calling, and commissioning of the Twelve are merely aspects of Jesus' relationship with them. Rather, according to Barth's explication, as examination of some further portions of his expository work makes clear, Jesus' appointment, calling, and commissioning of the apostles constitute his specific relationship with the apostles and, by way of them, with all others.

## Commissioning (C.D. IV/2, pp. 207-9)

Commenting on Romans 10:14ff., Barth remarks, "The problem of the salvation of men, of their calling on the name of the Lord, of their faith in Him, of their hearing of His Word, is clearly the existence or non-existence of preachers" (p. 207). If we pay close attention to the text of Romans 10, the problem of these preachers themselves is that of their "sending." To understand what preaching and kerygma are and are not, we need to observe the action and word of those who follow Jesus in the New Testament. "They can be preachers only as (in the narrower and wider sense of the term) they are 'apostles', *i.e.*, men who are sent" (p. 207). Their "commissioning" means that they must start from the man Jesus as he was raised from the dead. They are witnesses of his resurrection and are commissioned to proclaim it. "This commissioning is the possibility and power of their κηρύσσειν with all the consequences of this action for the hearing, faith, confession and salvation of them who are nigh and them that are afar off" (p. 208). It is the power of his resurrection to which they give witness and which in turn is the power of their witness. As their witness is a participant in this power, it is effective unto faith and salvation.

But these apostles do not come from heaven. If it is Jesus in his resurrection (the man Jesus manifested in the mode of God) who reveals to them that his existence with them and action for them is *for all*, then it is *the specific existence he lived with them* that is to be proclaimed to all. Or, to say it another way, if the power of the apostles' preaching is the power of Jesus' resurrection, its content remains his specific relationship with them — the specific relationship that they learned as his pupils by his appointment — now made effective for all. "These twelve Jesus sent out, charging them . . . [to] preach . . . , saying, 'The Kingdom of heaven is at hand' (Matthew 10:5 & 7)" (p. 208). This proclamation, first on the lips of John the Baptist, then on the lips of Jesus, and in a preliminary way on the lips of the apostles, is placed effectively on the lips of the apostles by the power of Jesus' resurrection.

Thus Barth draws our attention to the overlapping of the commissioning and appointment of the apostles. Power is given their preaching by their being made participants in the power of Jesus' resurrection (their commissioning), but its content is to be their account of their relationship with Jesus as his appointed pupils. How can Jesus in the earlier stage of their specific relationship with him become superfluous? Their preaching (which is the good news of accomplished salvation declared to their hearers) indeed occurs because he sends them to preach; their preaching is the execution of his commission to them. But the content of their preaching takes up and reproduces Jesus' proclamation to them.

This relationship of Jesus with the apostles is what is given effective power (for both the apostles and their hearers) by Jesus' commissioning of the apostles. Insofar as commissioning is the empowering of their appointment, it can be said that "the power of [the apostles'] action lies in [their] relationship [with Jesus]. It is because of this relationship that there can be said of them and their work: 'He who hears you hears me' (Luke 10:16). As they speak from this relationship, they are authorized . . . and need not fear anyone or anything. Without this relationship [the Word of the apostles] would be nothing" (p. 208). There is no immanent power or value or salvation in the preacher or in his preaching or even in the Christian kerygma. Such a notion "is one of the most monstrous mythologoumena of all times" (p. 208). The preaching of the apostles is the preaching or account of their specific relationship with Jesus, which by the power of his resurrection is inclusive of all others.

## Calling (C.D. II/2, pp. 623-30)

At a critical point Barth's exposition of Mark 10:17-31 (the story of Jesus' relationship with the rich young man) turns, as does the text (vv. 23-24), to Jesus' relationship with the apostles. Peter declares to Jesus, "Lo, we have left everything and followed you" (v. 28). Jesus does not contradict Peter, but rather assures him and the other disciples that they are on the way to eternal life (vv. 29-30). Should we assume, then, that the apostles, unlike the rich young man, are those who obey the command "Come, follow me"? Jesus does not draw this conclusion, nor do the disciples. Rather, we read that they were "amazed" (v. 24) and "exceedingly astonished" (v. 26a) at Jesus' words about how hard it is to enter the kingdom of God. They wonder, "Who, then, can be saved?" (v. 26b). The disciples have done, and therefore can do, what is necessary. What then prompts their amazement and astonishment? Did all they had left behind to follow Jesus still loom before them and hinder their obedience to him?

What they saw, according to Barth's explication of this passage, is how greatly difficult a step of obedience to Jesus is and how, once taken, it must be taken again and again. Their solidarity with the disobedient has been made evident to them; that is, in relation to Jesus they are in the same position as the rich young man. "According to the saying of Jesus in vs. 27 even that they — the obedient — should be saved is impossible with men. . . . From the point of view of their own ability [the disciples], too, lack everything [the rich young man] lacked" (p. 625). But Jesus is obedient for them — and he attributes, in prospect of his intercession, his ability in obedience to them. They are disobedient apart from this attribution, which is his calling of them. And because they are called they must apply their acquittal (made good in his intercession) not only to themselves, but also to the rich young man in prospect of his future obedience to his calling, which applications give to both them and him the promise of eternal life. If the grace of Jesus is there for the disciples, how can it fail to be present for the rich young man and for all the others who, like them, lack the ability of obedience in themselves? The only advantage that the disciples have over the rich young man is that Jesus *makes known* to them that his ability in obedience is attributed to them (although Jesus makes this effectively known to them only, after his intercession, by his resurrection). "Made obedient and set on the way to eternal life, in relation to all other men [the disciples] are witnesses to the fact that what they are permitted to be and do is the will of God for [other men] too, and that possibility by which they themselves live is given to [other men] too, and may be used by them" (p. 627).

The conclusion of this story ("many that are first will be last, and the last first," v. 31), according to Barth's explication, makes clear that everything that has taken place between Jesus and the rich young man on the one side and the apostles on the other involves a threat of judgment for the disciples and a promise for the rich young man. The apostles are still looking back to what was left behind in their concern, "What is to become of us?" The inability of the apostle for obedience is exposed. He is depicted as one who has no capacity for his relationship of obedience to Jesus. But Jesus addresses the disciples as men who have left everything behind for his sake and the Gospel's and are worthy of the eternal reward (vv. 29-30). Does Jesus not recognize that Peter, their spokesman, in looking back to what they left behind, has denied what they are in relation to Jesus? Indubitably he does. "But in His answer Jesus steps, as it were, over that abyss for them and with them — again making them, from what they are in themselves, into what they are permitted to be by and with Him" (p. 629). He addresses his disciples not according to what they are in themselves — anxious and disobedient — but according to what they are by the strength of his calling them to be apostles. "In face of their scarcely concealed defection, Jesus becomes and is again, and this time truly, Jesus the Saviour. . . . They are relieved of their concern by the fact that Jesus takes it on Himself. And it is as He intercedes for them that the promise He gives them becomes powerful and decisive" (p. 629). The promise to the disciples and the act of intercession for them (which coincide in this episode), in prospect of their fulfillment in Jesus' death and exaltation, cut the ground out from under the disciples' anxiety (disobedience and disloyalty) and their calling is made sure. That their calling is made sure in them is demonstrated by the fact that subsequent to their commissioning "what has been said and done in their favour by Jesus, the disciples cannot refrain from repeating in favour of [the rich young man] and those like him, and with the same indefatigability as Jesus devoted to them" (p. 630). Yet the sureness of their calling does not place it beyond threat, but precisely under threat, howbeit a salutary threat ("the first shall be last"). Exactly because they are called, they are made responsible to their call. They are called away from "looking back" on "everything left behind," and they stand in need of again and again hearing and heeding this call from the person Jesus, who binds them to himself by it.

## *Appointment (C.D. II/2, pp. 459-506)*

While not concentrating directly upon the appointment of the Twelve in his exposition of the New Testament texts concerning the relation of Jesus and Judas, Barth's exposition of those texts brings into relief the specific character of their appointment.[4] For while in the case of the eleven appointment, calling, and commissioning interpenetrate each other, that is not so in the case of Judas Iscariot. For Judas, although appointed, is not commissioned. And while Jesus' intercessory death takes place first of all for the Twelve, and therefore for Judas, since Judas never proclaims this death as his acquittal, we must also say that his calling was not exercised. Yet he was clearly appointed an apostle

---

4. Only this aspect of Barth's expository discussion of the relationship between Jesus and Judas will receive attention in this section.

and was an apostle. What he does, then, casts light on the appointment of the apostle.

Judas Iscariot is undoubtedly an apostle — no less so than Peter and John, sharing with them the same appointment. He is mentioned by name in all of the New Testament lists of the Twelve. All three of the Synoptic Gospels speak of "Judas, one of the twelve" (Mark 14:43; Matt. 26:47; Luke 22:47), and John depicts Jesus saying directly to the disciples, " 'Have I not chosen you, the twelve, and one of you is a devil?' He spoke of Judas the son of Simon Iscariot, for he, one of the twelve, was to betray him" (John 6:70-71). When the gospel story recounts Jesus' relationship with the disciples, what he said to them and did for them, Judas is present among them playing a passive and active role. "He was numbered among us, and was allotted his share in this ministry" (Acts 1:17). And he ate and drank at the Last Supper with Jesus and the others. "None of the Synoptists denied that Judas also received that which Jesus gave to the apostles at the institution of the Lord's Supper" (p. 459). The Gospel account does not declare that Judas had only the appearance of an apostle, but rather makes it plain that he was one of the genuine apostles.

The act which characterizes Judas' apostleship is the act of "handing over" Jesus. Jesus had created a sphere in which he ruled — the sphere of his free utterance and work, the sphere of the apostolate — from which Judas delivered him into the hands of men. Judas' act is the first link in the chain — he hands over Jesus to the high priests, they hand over Jesus to the Gentiles in the person of Pontius Pilate, who hands over Jesus for crucifixion. While this description of the work of the appointed apostle is clearly meant to be the negative parallel of the positive handing over of Jesus to Israel and to the Gentiles by the apostolate in the execution of its appointment and commission after Jesus' ascension, Barth (in making this observation) also observes that the whole apostolate is represented in Judas' act and shares his guilt. Between Jesus' sphere, the sphere of the twelve apostles, and the world there has to be this relation too — of shared guilt. "The whole significance of the apostolate, of the choosing of the twelve apostles, depends upon the fact that this happened" — that Jesus was "handed over" by Judas (p. 461). Judas and the other apostles belong together — with all the closeness with which Jesus chose and appointed them (p. 471). What Judas did any of the other eleven could have done (Mark 14:19; Matt. 26:22; Luke 22:23; John 13:22ff.). Jesus objectively cleansed all of the apostles, including Judas, in gathering and appointing them and in being present with them. He objectively washed them by "gathering them to Himself and making them witnesses of His acts and hearers of His Word. . . . [Their cleansing] consists in the fact that Jesus called them His own and was with them as His own . . . [establishing] the relationship between them and Himself" (p. 472).

However, the effectiveness of this objective cleansing awaits its completion in Jesus' death and its manifestation in Jesus' resurrection.[5] "The effectiveness" of this objective cleansing refers to its intended goal: the reception by the apostle of Jesus as the One to whom he belongs. Judas shows what the apostles — appointed but not yet effectively called (by Jesus' intercessory death) and commissioned (in the power of Jesus' resurrection) — still lack. "It is because Judas is among them, because the presence and act of this apostle show what is involved in the fact that all the apostles are 'in the world,' that Jesus must die for the sake of this uncleanness and its removal" (p. 474). What Judas shows — that Jesus' objective cleansing of the apostles needs to become effective for them — is no less true for Peter than for Judas. "The basic flaw was revealed in Judas, but it was that of the apostolate as a whole" (p. 475). This subjective flaw (on the apostles' side of the relationship) required a judgment upon them, notwithstanding the objective cleansing (from Jesus' side of the relationship) of their appointment. And this judgment, which they all incurred with Judas, Jesus takes upon himself for them in his death. His death is the effective washing of all the disciples.[6]

Judas' act could not invalidate his appointment as an apostle. He does not exercise it properly, but it is still there — even as a *locum tenens* in Paul's reference to the Twelve in 1 Corinthians 15:5, where there could be no question of Matthias or Paul himself, a *locum tenens* that Paul himself fills according to the implication of Acts (p. 477).[7] Paul, like Judas,[8] hands over Jesus to the Gentiles, not now in unfaithfulness, not now aiming at Jesus' death, but rather aiming at making

---

5. That Barth recognizes that Jesus' death is, in the first place, for the apostles he indicates when he says, "Jesus does not give [the sacrifice of His life] into the void when He gives it in death. He gives it to them [the disciples]" (p. 474).

6. Judas does not avail himself of it.

7. The implication rests on the preponderant attention given in Acts to the ministry of Paul.

8. Judas' "handing over" of Jesus is the first link in the chain in which Jesus is handed over to the Gentiles, who, in the person of Pontius Pilate, deliver him to be crucified.

known the Lordship of this One who was slain but is risen. Judas was not able to nullify the appointment to apostleship. When he fell, his replacement began the true story of the apostles' genuine handing over of Jesus to the Gentiles.

In Barth's exposition this replacement by Paul of Judas among the Twelve brings into relief what belongs to the apostles' appointment. For the manifestation of the man Jesus of Nazareth *in the mode of God* to Paul on the road to Damascus is clearly enough his *commissioning*. And this manifestation was, at once, the manifestation to Paul of *the man Jesus,* crucified and risen. In this manifestation (and its aftermath) the crucified and risen Jesus converts Paul from sinful rejecter of him to faithful proclaimer of the forgiveness of sins and new life in him (to which Paul's own life is made witness). The same Damascus road event bespeaks, then, Paul's *calling* as well as his commissioning. And since his calling and commissioning are direct acts of Jesus, he, no less than the other apostles (in the narrower sense of the word) is called and commissioned directly by Jesus.[9] But only Paul's enrollment in Judas' place (which is not explicitly mentioned in the New Testament) makes clear his appointment.[10]

Barth's introduction of the topic of Judas' appointment and Paul's exercise of it into his discussion of the apostolate does not lead away from the already presented results of his exposition: namely, that Jesus' appointment, calling, and commissioning of the Twelve is what constitutes them apostles, and that (contrary to any Gnostic attempt to promote a diffusion of Jesus) it is Jesus' gathering, upholding, and sending of the Twelve by which he gathers, upholds, and sends many (or all) others. But the discussion becomes more complex when it is

9. According to Barth's exposition all Christians are appointed, called, and commissioned. But all Christians, subsequent to the Twelve, are appointed, called, and commissioned by Jesus' inclusion of them in his appointment, calling, and commissioning of the Twelve. This is not true of Paul who, according to Barth, is one of the Twelve. I also might note that Barth maintains that not only Christians but all people are objectively included by Jesus in his appointment, calling, and commissioning of the Twelve. Their subjective inclusion is determined in "the open situation of proclamation."

10. The reader is reminded (cf. n. 4 above) that this section is not a résumé of Barth's expository discussion of Jesus and Judas in *C.D.* II/2, pp. 459-506. Rather, I want to focus attention upon what in Barth's exposition bears upon the appointment of the apostles and, at this point, its implications for that topic. The emphasis on the point that Paul does not receive a direct appointment from Jesus is mine. (However, Barth implies this point.) Reference to what Barth says elsewhere about appointment (cf. Chapter One) is being taken into account.

said (or implied) that Judas received his appointment from Jesus, but received neither effective calling nor commissioning, and when it is further said that explicitly in New Testament texts Paul received effective calling and commissioning, both of which he executes, but that there is no explicit text that depicts his appointment. Taking account of this complexity could prove fruitful. For the lack of an explicit text depicting or referring to Paul's appointment prompts the question of whether Paul executed the task that appointment enjoins. This is the question about the material content of appointment, and to ask it should lead us into a more precise knowledge of its character.

Earlier I recounted Barth's description of appointment as enrollment of the pupil in the teacher's school.[11] The disciples are to teach what Jesus said and did — to "hand over" this Jesus to Jews and Gentiles. Judas executed this task in an alien fashion. Judas, a witness of what Jesus said and did, renouncing what Jesus said and did for him, handed over Jesus to his enemies. He handed over a freely acting person to those who would confine his freedom of activity. Judas brings to an end Jesus' freedom to preach the kingdom of God and to enact it in works. In consequence of Judas' act, Jesus can only suffer what his enemies inflict upon him. The preaching of the kingdom of God had been futile in its impact on Judas. Judas had been appointed to bring sinners under the power of Jesus, but had brought Jesus under the power of sinners (p. 481).

While Judas' "handing over" of Jesus is the description of an alien execution of apostolic appointment, nevertheless "handing over" is also the term used to describe the proper execution of apostolic appointment. The apostles are appointed to "hand over" to others, who had not directly witnessed them, an account of the words and deeds and death and resurrection of Jesus (p. 482). "It is necessary that Jesus Himself should . . . become the subject of the 'traditions of men'" with all the attendant dangers (p. 482). For it is the unsubstitutable Jesus in his specific relationship with the apostles, who wills to be the Lord of all men and women by gathering them into this specific relationship he had and has with the apostles. Jesus wills to be "handed over" by his apostles. And the risen Jesus, says Barth, does not fear this, for in this "handing over" he upholds (calls) and empowers (commissions) his apostles, constituting this delivery a redemptive delivery. What the apostle has redemptively received for himself, he delivers to others.

11. See Chapter One above.

Paul three times refers to his execution of the task of appointment. (1 Cor. 11:2: "I delivered the tradition to you"; 1 Cor. 15:3: "I delivered to you as of first importance what I received"; 1 Cor. 11:23: "For I received from the Lord what I also delivered to you." This last reference might be very nearly a claim to direct appointment, but is not unambiguously so.) An apostle is appointed to deliver an account of what Jesus did in front of and in relation to the disciples. Executing the task of appointment is so critical to Paul that, according to Barth's exposition of Paul's letters, "Everything further that [Paul] has to say to [his hearers] can consist only in a sharper repetition of this act, in an explanation and application of what he has delivered to them as an apostle" (p. 483). "[The apostles] do not speak as thinkers, but as eye witnesses and servants of the Word which has encountered them in Jesus Christ and to the claim of which they are subject" (p. 498). Paul fulfills the task of an appointed disciple: He hands over an account of what Jesus said and did and of what befell him.

But the matter of Paul's appointment is not resolved by saying that he fulfilled the task of an appointed disciple. For Paul is not explicitly appointed and this is not a semantic quibble. The Twelve were appointed to be witnesses of Jesus in his Galilean ministry and in his passion and death in Jerusalem. Judas was an eyewitness of these events, Paul was not. Paul shares with the eleven Jesus' direct calling and commissioning, as Judas does not, but he is not directly appointed as were the Twelve.

Barth directs our attention at this point to Judas. Judas is appointed to deliver what Jesus said and did, and in alien fashion he does so. He renounces what Jesus said to him and did for him by delivering Jesus, the person of these words and acts, to his enemies. Judas enacts his evil intention. But Judas, serving God against his own intention, also enacted God's good intention in the same act. The good intention of God makes the act of Jesus' crucifixion good, therein nullifying the consequence of Judas' enacted intention (p. 504). (The intention of Judas, of course, is still evil, even if the consequence he intended is made void.) Thus, it is not the case that God merely renders the consequence of Judas' evil intention void. He does so by employing positively for his service Judas' alien work of apostolic appointment, by making the consequence of Judas' act, Jesus' death, salvific. Yet that is not all that must be said. For God wills not merely to confirm in this way Judas' appointment as an apostle, even in its alien execution, but also wills that the proper execution of his appointment not go unfulfilled. There is one who is not appointed, but in whom the dead Judas exists (p. 504). And this other, in whom the dead Judas exists, is first to be observed in his continuation of Judas' alien work of "handing over." For Paul is, first, zealous in delivering up those who were "handing over" Jesus. In the first instance, however, Paul is to be distinguished from Judas. For Judas began from within the apostolic sphere and Paul begins from without. And Judas is never without, never not an apostle, never not one of the Twelve. He retains his appointment. Yet Paul by virtue of Jesus' direct calling and direct commissioning is brought into the apostolic sphere. But not by appointment. How can he give an account of Jesus' ministry in Galilee and passion in Jerusalem? Yet God "mysteriously" equips him to deliver the tradition.[12] Paul is not appointed, but rather executes, now properly, *Judas'* appointment. While Paul is directly called and commissioned by Jesus, his proper execution of apostolic appointment is God's grace making good in him Judas' default on his appointment.

12. "Mysteriously" has reference here to Galatians 1:11–2:10. It would be a remarkable exegete who could finally resolve what Paul means when he says, "For I did not receive [the Gospel] from man, nor was I taught it, but it came through a revelation of Jesus Christ" or when he says he "did not confer with flesh and blood, nor did I go up to Jerusalem to those who were apostles before me" or when he says, "those . . . who were of repute added nothing to me." However one understands these verses, precisely because Paul delivers the tradition it cannot be thought that in these statements he is supporting a notion of a vague diffusion of Christ to those who come after the time of Jesus' ministry in Galilee and passion in Jerusalem, thereby bypassing the "handing over" of the account of Jesus' relationship with the apostles. (The comment is mine, not Barth's.)

# 3 The Definiteness
of Christ's Presence
and Its Hermeneutical Clue

Frei attends to the specific identity that Jesus enacts in the gospel story. Jesus enacted his identity in relation to God and, in turn, is manifested in that identity as the presence of God. However, Frei leaves unattended the specific identity that Jesus enacted in his relationship with the apostles. Since, as Frei demonstrates, the only way to speak of Jesus' presence is by way of speaking of his identity, Frei's inattention to Jesus' relationship with the apostles leads him into a discussion of Jesus' presence that is deficient regarding its specificity.

In this chapter I will review Frei's account of Jesus' presence,[1] Barth's account of the definiteness of Jesus' presence and, finally, will make a brief comparison of these two accounts with a view to the discussion of biblical interpretation in the following chapter.

## Frei on the Presence of Jesus Christ

Because it belongs to Jesus' identity to be a particular man who is, at once, the presence of God, Jesus cannot not be. To acknowledge his identity is to acknowledge that he cannot not be present. "The climax of the Gospel story is the full unity of the unsubstitutable individuality of Jesus with the presence of God" (p. 154). But to say this kind of thing, Frei remarks, is not yet to say anything specifically about his presence. How are we to speak specifically about Jesus' presence to us?

1. *Identity,* chap. 14.

**41**

Frei's concentration on Jesus' identity, as described in the Gospels, provides the basis for his discussion of Jesus' presence to us. Since Jesus has an unsubstitutable identity other humans have an unsubstitutable identity too. Jesus gained this for them. Even if Frei does not develop this point, he nevertheless makes it; and it is clear in his discussion that when we speak of Jesus' presence to us there will be no talk of merging identities.

When Frei turns to a discussion of the presence of Jesus Christ now, "in contrast to his presence at the time of his earthly life, death and resurrection, as well as in contrast to his final presence in a future mode" (p. 155), he speaks of the Holy Spirit. What is meant "by this term is described, first of all, by the complex unity of . . . the unsubstitutably human figure, Jesus of Nazareth, and the presence and action of God. . . . The climax of the Gospel story involves an insistence that from now on we can no longer think of God except as we think of Jesus at the same time nor of Jesus except by reference to God" (p. 155). Frei does not proffer a definition of the Holy Spirit, but rather indicates that the term or name denotes that the presence of God now is the presence of Jesus now. The Holy Spirit is the mode of Jesus' presence now. But since Jesus is not present now as he was to his disciples in his earthly life, death, and resurrection, that is, tangibly, audibly, visibly, nor as he shall be in his final presence in the future mode, his presence now is indirect. While Jesus' presence now is the presence of one whose identity is such that he cannot be conceived as not present, yet we cannot directly conceive it. To conceive his indirect presence now requires a temporal and spatial basis, for if we can only conceive direct presence in terms of physical presence and verbal communication, so we will have to conceive indirect presence in terms of an analogy to physical presence and verbal communication. The Word (Scripture and expository preaching) and sacrament are the temporal and spatial bases for Jesus' indirect presence. Frei adds the cautionary statement that the presence of Jesus Christ is not subject to the confinement of its freedom by Word and sacrament (p. 155).

In speaking of the Holy Spirit, Christians, Frei continues, affirm the strange unity of factual affirmation and dispositional commitment in the believer's response to Jesus' presence. To know Jesus' identity is to affirm that he is present and to adore him — indeed, for the believer, they are one and the same thing. Just as Jesus' identity and presence cannot be conceived apart, so factual affirmation of his presence and adoration of it cannot be conceived apart in the believer's response to that presence.[2]

Frei speaks not only of the Word and sacraments as the temporal and spatial bases of Jesus Christ's presence now, that presence being called the Holy Spirit, and of the believer's response of factual affirmation and dispositional commitment to that presence, but he also refers to the church. The church not only witnesses to that presence but also is "the public and communal form the indirect presence of Christ now takes" (p. 157). How does Frei move from an explication of the Gospels as identity descriptions of Jesus Christ to these statements about the Word and sacraments as the temporal and spatial bases of Christ's presence now and of the church as the form of Christ's presence now? He explains that the schemata of identity description he applied to Jesus in the Gospels must in an analogous way be applied to the church. In applying these schemata of identity description to the church Frei, first, indicates that the relation between Jesus Christ and the church is somewhat like that of the relation between Jesus Christ and Israel. To describe Israel is to narrate its history. And to identify that people with Jesus, as the New Testament does, means to narrate Jesus' history as the individual and climactic summing up and identification of the whole people in such wise that Israel receives its identification from him. Likewise the church moves toward a climactic summing up of its history that must be narrated, but cannot yet be because its history is unfinished. The church is thus the subject of a history. This subject is constituted by the Word and sacraments. While Frei appears to say that this subject, church, is identical with the indirect presence of Christ, that is, with the Holy Spirit, he quickly dissipates this appearance by

---

2. To elucidate this point Frei refers to the temptation to separate factual affirmation and commitment. Doctrinaire Christians fall prey to insisting on the factual affirmation and self-centeredly escape from the claim of love. They become defensive in the way in which they hold on to doctrine. Other believers, in their doubt, will associate themselves with humane causes, claiming that this advocacy is the proper response to Christ's presence. But the support of humane causes may have many impulses and without the factual affirmation the ambiguous association of Jesus' presence with human sensitivity will seem half-hearted or even forced. In a similar way the church can fall prey to temptation. The church affirms the temporal and spatial bases of Christ's indirect presence *in unity* with his presence in and to the shape of public events. The church may be tempted on the one hand to sacramental or biblicist traditionalism. On the other hand it may, in moral activism arising out of passionate concern for the world, fail to do justice to the indispensability of Word and sacraments.

saying "it is obvious that this understanding of the church as a 'subject self' is analogous to rather than identical with the subject self that is Jesus" (p. 159).

Frei goes on to apply the intention-action pattern of identity description to the church as he did to Jesus. (We recall that according to this pattern identity is constituted by the interaction of character and circumstances and thus must be narrated. A subject is who he is in the enactment of his most central intentions within the circumstances in which he finds himself. The same descriptive pattern is applicable to the subject: church.) "The intention-action pattern of the story of the church differs from that of Jesus in two respects" (p. 160). First, the church is a follower of Jesus, not a reiteration of him.[3] Like him it serves, rather than being served,[4] but unlike him it receives enrichment from its neighbor (the world at large). Second, the church's intention-action pattern, unlike Jesus', is unfinished. It yet looks to Jesus' presence in a future mode. "Just as Jesus was at once an individual person and event and yet also the climactic summary and incorporation of that history which is the people Israel, so the future mode of that presence will be a significant, incorporative summing up of history in a manner that we should be fools to try to imagine or forecast in a literal fashion" (pp. 160-61).

In indicating Jesus' connection with all others, Frei introduces the word *history*, about which he briefly speaks.

> History is not to be equated with a series of cultural perspectives, or with a moment of decision in which a self takes a stance of "openness" toward what will happen in any case in an unending series, regardless of what kind of action might be appropriate. Nor is history some . . . hidden portent within public occurrences. History is public history — the intention-action pattern formed by the interaction of the church with mankind at large; and it is this history which forms the mysterious pattern of meaning to be disclosed by the presence of God in Jesus Christ in the future mode. . . . This presence to history means that history is neither chaotic nor fated, but providentially ordered in the life, death and resurrection of Jesus Christ, who is Lord of the past, the present and the future. (P. 161)

3. In the present work it is argued that the church is a reiteration of the apostolate.
4. Frei here refers to "the pattern of exchange" in Jesus' life and death.

History, again, is public history — "the intention-action pattern formed by the church's interaction with mankind at large."

It is in this context of history that Frei speaks of the Word and sacraments as the temporal and spatial bases for Christ's indirect presence now and of the church as the public form of that indirect presence now. The Word and the sacraments and the church are ingredient in his description of history, which is providentially ordered in the life, death, and resurrection of Jesus. Frei does not, then, seek to confine the indirect presence of Jesus Christ to the church and to the Word and sacraments. World is ingredient in church, just as church is ingredient in world. "In the instance of the church, reference to the Spirit means affirmation of the spatial, temporal bases of Christ's indirect presence in unity with his presence in and to the shape of public events of the world and of human history. The church is constituted by the one [Jesus' presence by, although not identical with, the temporal and spatial bases] . . . as well as by the other (his presence to the course of human history) and by their unity" (pp. 157-58).

Frei does not seek *the* clue to the pattern of history, but allows that we may, by reference to the Word, reach for parables of the indirect presence of Jesus Christ that take place in the history of the interaction of the church with humanity at large.[5] He speaks of Paul's declaration in Romans 11 of how God has chosen the Gentiles in and by his rejection of Israel and of how this shall finally redound to Israel's salvation. Parabolically, the really significant events for the church may well transpire in humankind outside the church from which the latter will receive its enrichment. "Humanity at large is the neighbour given to the church, through whom Christ is present to the church" (p. 162). Other parables might be discerned in light of Jesus' death on the cross, which brought about a union of radical opposites (enemies) through an agonized exchange. "All terrible sacrifices dimly set forth the same pattern" (p. 162). Frei sets in this light the sacrifices made in the American Civil War, the civil rights struggle in the United States, and the suffering inflicted upon the Vietnamese people by the Americans. We can reach for these parables, because there will be a summing up of history. Just as Jesus in his passion and resurrection was the summation of Israel's history, so Jesus in the final mode of his presence will be the summation of the history of the interaction of the church with humanity at large.

5. This point will be elucidated later in this chapter; see the section entitled "Frei: Living in the Word."

And the present interaction of life in the church with the world is the token and pledge of this hope. But the history of providence must be narrated. It is mysterious, not mechanical. God's work is mysteriously coexistent with the contingency of events (p. 163). There is no scientific rule to describe it. Indeed, when thinking of God's providential rule, which is ordered to the life, death, and resurrection of Jesus, "the believer must abide by the New Testament's complex rather than simple identification of God and Jesus — an identification which can only be narrated" (p. 164), an identification that arises from both the unity and distinctiveness of God and Jesus in the resurrection appearances.

This is the context in which Frei intends to place his discussion of the temporal and spatial bases of Christ's indirect presence now. If the clues to God's providential activity are inferred from the gospel story, the same story directly witnesses the complex relation of God and Jesus. The gospel story with its full biblical context is the Word, and this Word is explicated in preaching and sacrament. The person this Word describes, Jesus, points away from himself to God. But this witness, Jesus, who points away from himself to God, is witnessed by the very God to whom he witnesses. By analogy the Word, Scripture and expository preaching, witnesses to Jesus Christ and Jesus Christ indirectly witnesses to it; he makes himself present to it so that it becomes the temporal basis of the Spirit, who is the indirect presence of Jesus Christ. Similarly, the spatial basis for the indirect presence of Christ now is the sacrament, in which Christ communicates himself to us, not physically, but in an analogous physical form, since we cannot know self-focused presence except in physical form. "To the believer, the verbal and spatial bases of Christ's presence are the compelling means by which God's presence in Jesus Christ comes to be identical with his effective act of self-presentation now" (p. 165).

## Commentary

Frei's literal ascriptive exposition of the gospel story is clear and cogent and its influence upon biblical hermeneutics has demonstrated its fruitfulness.[6] Yet a lacuna is present in it that needs attention, not least of all because of its bearing upon biblical hermeneutics. The lacuna becomes

6. Ingredient in Frei's influence is also his demonstration in *Eclipse* of the questionableness of "non-literal ascriptive" explications of Scripture.

evident when Frei speaks of Jesus' presence now. But it occurs already in his description of Jesus' identity, when he leaves out of account Jesus' relationship with his apostles, a relationship ingredient in Jesus' identity. Frei adequately demonstrates the initial propositions he formulates about Jesus' presence: (1) given who Jesus is, he cannot not be present; (2) the only possible order in speaking of Jesus' identity and presence is to begin with his identity and only then speak of his presence. But Frei moves from these initial and well-grounded propositions to a discussion of Jesus' indirect presence now which he specifies in terms of its temporal and spatial bases in Word and sacraments and in terms of the church in the context of history. ("History" is the public occurrence of the interaction of church and world providentially ordered to the life, death, and resurrection of Jesus, an ordering to be manifested by Jesus in a future mode.) A lacuna has opened between Frei's expository description of Jesus' identity and his description of Jesus' indirect presence now; that is, between, on the one hand, Frei's description of Jesus' identity and, on the other hand, his discussion of Word and sacrament as witnesses to, and of the church as the communal form of, Christ's indirect presence now and of his application of identity description schemata to the church in history. That is not to say that all of these discussions do not belong to a consideration of Jesus' presence now. But a lacuna has opened between the identity description of Jesus and such discussions about his presence now. And this is not merely a technical problem. Quite the contrary, for this lacuna gives rise to a too indefinite description of Jesus' presence and affects the way in which Scripture is interpreted.

The lacuna arises from inattention to Jesus' relationship with the apostles and to the apostles' relationship with Jesus. If the Gospels are exponents of Jesus' appointment, calling, and commissioning of the apostles, then the texts belong to the event of the apostles being gathered, upheld, and commissioned by Jesus; and in this is their unity. The unity of the other biblical books with the Gospels will be understood in terms of their inclusion by way of expectation or recollection in the event or movement of Jesus' appointment, calling, and commissioning of the apostles. If the biblical texts and their unity are not conceived in this fashion, then their unity may be conceived to be of a literary order, to be discerned by espying a literary pattern of typology or figuration in them. This is not to say, of course, that figuration or typology is not employed in the biblical texts. But this literary device is employed in function of the event of Christ's gathering, upholding, and sending his own. This is the unvarying form of Christ's presence, consonant with his identity. And it is precisely here that Frei provides insufficient ground. That is not to say that he provides no ground at all. Scarcely that. For, despite the lacuna in his presentation, he provides the most fundamental ground for speaking of Jesus' presence when he says "that the climax of the Gospel story involves the insistence that from now on we can no longer think of God except we think of Jesus at the same time, nor of Jesus except by reference to God" (p. 155). It is only that Frei fails to specify this Jesus as the One who gathered, upheld, and sent his apostles and who is never present except as the One who indefatigably continues to gather, uphold, and send many (or all) others by including them in his appointment, calling, and commissioning of the Twelve.

## Barth on the Definiteness of Christ's Presence

### *The Gathering of the Christian Community*[7]

The coming of Jesus Christ in his ministry, passion, and resurrection is the divine act. Ingredient in this act is Jesus' choosing of certain men to participate in it both actively and passively. The fact that there are also men and women who are chosen for active and passive participation in Jesus' coming after the time of Jesus' ministry, passion, and resurrection is a new thing — and yet not a new thing. It is new insofar as it belongs to the story of Christ's coming in which each event is unique and has its own integrity; it is not new insofar as the gospel story had in view from the very first as its provisional end the apostolic story.[8] Indeed, while the apostolic story is distinct from the gospel story it is comprehensible for faith only as it is enclosed in the gospel story, finding its origin and goal in it.[9] The power by which Jesus Christ

---

7. Material from two paragraphs of the *Church Dogmatics* is presented in this and the next subsection: first from "The Holy Spirit and the Gathering of the Christian Community" (IV/1) and second from "The Definiteness of the Divine Decision" (II/2). Only the material in those paragraphs pertinent to the topic of the definiteness of Christ's presence is reviewed.

8. In the wider sense of the word *apostolic*.

9. "The adding of the adjective 'Christian' to a human action — the action of the Christian community and the Christian individual — indicates that we are now dealing with man as he stands in a *particular* relationship to Jesus Christ" (*C.D.* IV/1, p. 644, italics added). The specificity of that particular relationship to Jesus Christ is the subject in Barth's theology that shall be unfolded in this subsection and the next.

encloses the story of men and women into his story, the power by which he includes later men and women into his relationship with the apostles, is the Holy Spirit. We would expect Barth, as we would expect any serious biblical expositor, to say this. What I wish to examine is his description of this "enclosing" activity of Jesus, which he performs in the power of the Holy Spirit.[10] To say description is not to say explanation. To speak of the power and presence of Jesus Christ in and to men and women who come after the time of his earthly ministry, death, and resurrection, we look forward in faith from Jesus Christ as the Gatherer, Upholder, and Sender of the apostles in the gospel story and backward from the existence of the gathered, upheld, and sent in the apostolic story (pp. 649-50).

The Christian community exists "only as it is gathered and lets itself be gathered and gathers itself by the living Jesus Christ through the Holy Spirit" (p. 650). The Christian community is an event; in the first instance, the event of being gathered and (in obedience) gathering.[11] While Barth aligns being "gathered" to "awakening" on the inner plane of the gathered, the terminology of being "gathered" bespeaks a public activity. As the apostles were "awakened" by the public teaching of Jesus and thereupon followed him, the Teacher, so, too, the awakening of the Christian coincides with his or her enrollment in the school of the apostles. "The predicate apostolic, and especially this predicate, describes the being of the community as an event" (p. 714). For the person who wants to recognize the community cannot do so as an observer outside of it, but must become a pupil in the apostles' school,

> himself hearing their witness, himself being taught and questioned by them. He must be put by them in a *definite movement,* in the movement in which they found themselves, in which they still find themselves today — for in the New Testament they are still before us in living speech and action. To be in the community of Jesus Christ means to take part in *this movement.* And it is and is known as the true Church by the fact that where it exists as such it finds itself in *this movement.* This movement is a very concrete but a spiritual process. It is definitely distinguished from other such movements. (P. 715, italics added)

10. We are interested in this topic particularly in its pertinence for biblical hermeneutics.
11. Its upholding and sending are also events.

Barth specifies the concreteness of this movement. "The earthly-historical medium of [Jesus'] self-manifestation is those in whose midst He has lived on earth, in history, as the Word of God made flesh. . . . These are the apostles. It is He Himself who has appointed and called and . . . sent them out for this purpose. . . . They . . . are His direct witnesses. . . . [In their witness the community] receives His own witness to Himself. Accepting the word of the apostles, [the community] allows Him to speak" (p. 718). This is not to say that the apostles are lords. Rather, Christ, who fashioned his relationship with the apostles and therein their relationship with him, fashions his relationship with the subsequent Christian community (and each of its members) and its relationship with him by including, in the power of the Holy Spirit, the community in his relationship with the apostles. Thus Christians are indefatigable students of the apostles' account of Christ's relationship with them. In this study is found what the church is and who the Christian is. What is magnified in this is, again, not the apostles themselves, but rather Christ's relationship with them; and it is this, not themselves, to which they attest. Having made that clear, Barth can say, "There is no way to Him which does not lead past them. . . . The awakening power of His Holy Spirit has no other earthly-historical form than that of the power of their witness" (p. 719).

The existence of the Christian community is the history of its encounter with and its explication and application (faithful and unfaithful) of the witness of the apostles. The relationship between Christ and both the Christian community and (therein) Christians is formed and not unformed, mediate and not immediate (p. 720). Its form corresponds to and replicates (howbeit in always new ways, because in new circumstances) the relationship of the apostles with Jesus Christ, or, if we wish to speak pointedly of Christ's presence, of the relationship of Christ with the apostles. The emphasis on relationship means that the church never "serves" the apostles, but him whom the apostles served and serve, in replication of their service.

> The Church finds itself in the school of the apostles [and] in this school it learns the meaning of obedience and practices obedience, making after them the movement of service which it sees them make — after them because they know immediately what it is all about. . . . In the measure that [the Church] does learn and practices [its *ministerium*] in this school [of the apostles] the Church acquires and has the true power which in exemplary form is effective and visible in the apostles as the servants of Jesus Christ, and therefore

[has] something of the power of the one great servant of God the attesting of whom has taught them obedience, who Himself is the man who instructs and guides and corrects and qualifies them in this school. It will never regret it if it enters this apostolic succession, if it remains in it, if it does not desire anything better, if it takes its part in it with a modesty and humility and yet also an attention and zeal which continually increase, if it becomes an apostolic community in this sense. (P. 720)

Again, in this section of the *Church Dogmatics,* Barth describes the apostles, but he now explicitly relates this description to that of the church. First, the apostles were gathered as the Twelve in correspondence with the twelve tribes of Israel. They represent in their person the inseparable connection of the new people of God with the old, and therein are a confirmation of the authority of the Old Testament (p. 721). Second, they were appointed to be the eyewitnesses of his words and acts and to what befell him. An apostle is one who has direct personal knowledge of Jesus Christ (p. 722).

Next, Barth speaks of their commissioning; the apostles are sent out to preach the gospel in the world (p. 724). But we should notice that they preach as ones who are called; that is, as ones who repose in Christ's intercession for them and not in their own rightness. "Their field is the world, and they are only sowers who pass over it. They renounce any self-grounded or self-reposing rightness or importance of their distinctive being and activity. . . . It cannot be otherwise than that . . . in this renunciation they should be a normative pattern to the community gathered by this ministry" (p. 724).

By correspondence to the existence and activity of the apostles later men and women are enclosed in the relationship of the apostles with Jesus. "As an apostolic Church the Church can never in any respect be an end in itself, but, following the existence of the apostles, it exists only as it exercises the ministry of a herald. . . . It cannot forget that it cannot do [what it does] for its own sake, but only in the course of its commission — only in an implicit and explicit outward movement to the world. . . . Its mission is not additional to its being. It is, as it is sent and active in its mission. It builds up itself for the sake of its mission and in relation to it" (p. 725).

Barth argues that Jesus' appointment, upholding, and commissioning of the apostolate are the means of his gathering, upholding, and sending of the Christian community and its individual members.

In this movement from the particular to the universal there is no loss of definiteness in Jesus' activity with and presence to his followers. Barth elucidates this point in his exposition of the Ten Commandments and the Sermon on the Mount. A scrutiny of this exposition can begin a deliberation about the implications of the definiteness of Jesus' relationship with his followers for biblical hermeneutics.

### The Definiteness of Jesus' Relationship with His Followers (C.D. II/2, pp. 672-708)

When we think of divine commands in the Bible we too readily "believe we have to do with lists of universal religious-moral-juridical rules and therefore with legal codes that are valid regardless of space and time" (p. 672). This "believing" is arbitrary in that "commands" in the Bible typically concern specific actions, attitudes, and achievements. "Nothing can be made of these commands if we try to generalize and transform them into universally valid principles. . . . Their content is purely concrete and related to this or that particular man in this or that particular situation. . . . They belong directly to a specific history, and they must be left in all their historical particularity and uniqueness" (pp. 672-73). A universally valid rule is not and cannot be a command. Up to the first edition of the Ten Commandments (Exod. 20:1ff.) and in the material immediately following it, there are no commands that could be made into universal principles.

Barth rehearses typical commands found in the Pentateuch: "Be fruitful, and multiply, and replenish the earth and subdue it" (Gen. 1:28) is the first command given to the first man and woman after creation and before the fall. The same command issued to Noah after the fall and flood already has a different form (Gen. 9:1ff.). In Genesis 2:16ff. the command is given the first man and woman not to eat of a certain tree. Noah is told how to build the ark (Gen. 6:14). Abraham is told to leave his country (Gen. 12:1) and to walk through the land of Canaan (Gen. 13:14ff.). In Genesis 15:9 Abraham is directed to make a specific sacrifice. Barth continues his rehearsal by referring to the specific directions given to Abraham (Gen. 17:10, 15), Lot (19:12), Abimelech (20:7), Isaac (26:2), Jacob (31:3; 46:3), Moses (Exod. 3:5; 4:3ff.; 4:19), and Aaron (4:27). In Exodus there are the institution of the Passover and the consecration of the first born (12:2ff.; 43ff.; 13:1), directions about how to cross the Red Sea (14:16ff.), instructions about the gathering of manna (16:4), and instructions to Moses about the rock in the wilderness and about unauthorized approach to Sinai (17:5; 19:12ff., 21ff.). "And this series of commands, as could easily be shown, continues throughout the Old Testament" (p. 674). These commands bespeak *ad hoc* actions and attitudes of an utterly definite character issued to specific persons in specific situations. These commands mean what they specifically say. The Ten Commandments appear in Barth's exposition anomalous.

"It is exactly the same in the New Testament" (p. 674). Barth rehearses the commands in Matthew's Gospel, leaving aside at first the material found in the Sermon on the Mount and other discourses, to repeat the point he made about commands in the Old Testament. Joseph is commanded to take Mary for his wife (1:20); to flee to Egypt with her (2:13); and to return from Egypt (2:20). Jesus directs John to baptize him (3:15). He commands Peter and John to leave their nets and come to him (4:19), the centurion at Capernaum to go his way (8:13), the man who wanted to bury his father to follow him instead (8:22), the demons to go into the swine (8:32), the sick of palsy to take up his bed and walk (9:6), Matthew to leave the tax office and follow him (9:9), the mourners in Jairus' house to depart (9:24), the man cured of blindness to keep silence about his cure (9:30), the disciples to keep silence about his messiahship (16:20), John's disciples to deliver a specific message to John (11:4-6), the man with the withered hand to stretch it forth (12:13), the disciples to give the crowd something to eat (14:16), Peter to come to him out of the boat (14:29), the father of the lunatic boy to bring the boy to him (17:17), Peter, James, and John to get up and not fear after they had fallen on their faces on the mountain of the transfiguration (17:7), the rich young man to sell all he had and give to the poor (19:21), the Pharisees and Herodians to pay their taxes to Caesar (22:21ff.), two disciples to bring an ass and her colt to him (21:2), the disciples to "take and eat" and "drink" (26:26-27) and to "watch and pray" (v. 41), and then to "rise" (v. 46), Peter to put up his sword (v. 52), Mary Magdalene and the other Mary not to be afraid and to tell "my brethren" to go to Galilee where they will see him (28:10). This is how Jesus spoke his commands to his disciples and to others. A rehearsal of the commands described in the other Gospels and in Acts and in a different way in the New Testament letters is of a piece with Matthew's account.

> The most important insights and decisions depend on these commands. None can be dispensed with. None is irrelevant. . . . None of them [is] less fortuitous, contingent, unique and involved in time

> and space than the commands of God in the Pentateuch. . . . Again, it is the case that those who want religious ethical principles will find nothing here, but will have to turn to other words of Jesus which seem to be more pregnant in this respect. Yet if they do they turn away from the living and acting person of Jesus Himself which is the content of the Gospel. . . . [Jesus] Himself and His will take the place of every universal precept. (P. 675)

Jesus, who is the divine Word of command, is present only in the definiteness of his relationship with his disciples and others surrounding them.

The divine command does not take the form of universal rules; Jesus issues concrete, definite orders. Human beings in a specific situation are commanded either to perform the specific act enjoined or to omit doing a specific act. The definiteness of these commands does not obscure but rather manifests their unity of purpose: the preparation and equipment of humans for the office of witness; or, more fully, that humans should be gathered and called to share in the community's ministry of witnessing (p. 678). The meaning of the specific commands, then, is not a general human meaning. Rather, Jesus commands a human to perform the unique and definite act that the unique and definite act of Christ's coming requires. "When Jesus commands and forbids, it means that He discloses His Messiahship and that He summons men to share either in His priestly or His kingly office, either exclusively as recipients or exclusively as those who are themselves to work and give" (p. 679).[12] It is because the divine person is so specific in both the Old Testament and the New Testament that the divine commands are so specific.

What does Barth make of the fact that there are in the Bible general rules that (1) appear to be directed to an indeterminate number of human beings and (2), being detached from specific circumstances, appear to be concerned not with specific actions but with possibilities of action on the part of all kinds of people? He argues that these texts are summaries of divine commands. They, in summary form, attest the sovereignty and character of him who issues concrete commands, the constitution of his community and the conditions and characteristics of those who belong to it. "[These summaries] concern [the people of

---

12. In this passage Barth, oddly, omits mention of Jesus' prophetic office and therefore an implied reference to appointment.

this community] because they are not just any men — as God is not just any being — but these particular men and women to whom God has specifically bound Himself and who for their part are specifically bound to God" (p. 682). They remind the members of the community that God will always continually claim them in the whole range of their life. They remind them of the holiness required by God of the members of his community, a holiness whose character they learn from the law handed on from generation to generation; a holiness they must know if they are to recognize the voice of the Good Shepherd and not harken unto the voice of a stranger. They provide, as it were, the background for the concrete commands Christ utters to his followers, providing a context by which to distinguish Christ's commands from other events. As background, or backdrop, they form the context for the events of the concrete commands and thus with them form a single whole (p. 683). This is why these summaries of the concrete commands are given, in Scripture, "the express form of definite historical events" (p. 683).

The Ten Commandments, then, are not direct commands, but only delimitations. They mark out the sphere of God's people in which God's concrete, positive directions are and will be issued (p. 684). The actual relationship between the Lord and his people is and will be determined by definite directions issued to specific persons in specific, concrete events of divine commanding and of human obedience or disobedience to these concrete directions. To keep the Ten Commandments is to take up the position of waiting for the specific command of the living God and to obey it when it occurs. All of this is made still clearer, Barth wants to show, when we turn to the Sermon on the Mount in Matthew's Gospel. Here and in the other great discourses in Matthew, Jesus defines the sphere in which he is present to his own, that is, to those whom he has appointed, called, and will call and commission in specific acts. His own can but desire to live in this sphere, for it is the sphere of Jesus' presence and activity and therefore of relationship with him who is the original and final point at issue in all human conduct (p. 688).

The divine act is the coming, intercession, and exaltation of Jesus. The Sermon on the Mount describes what his coming brings, the kingdom of God. Ingredient in his coming are Jesus' concrete commands uttered to the apostles, by which they are appointed to attest these words and deeds of his coming. But the kingdom of God is not merely the sphere in which Jesus' concrete commands occur, as if merely analogous to the sphere of holiness delineated by the Decalogue — a holiness that no concrete divine command will violate. For Jesus, the Proclaimer of the Word of command, is also the Intercessor for those who hear it. As he proclaims the Word and a man or woman hears it and believes it and lives in its strength, that man or woman is made righteous. "The righteousness of man required by the Sermon on the Mount consists objectively in the fact that Jesus recognizes him as His own, and subjectively in the fact that this righteous man belongs to Jesus, to the people which Jesus confesses in the judgment, which will not be condemned in the judgment (7:1), but will receive mercy (5:7)" (p. 692). What is commanded of a man or woman in the Sermon on the Mount is the confession that his or her righteousness depends upon Jesus' confession of him or her. This confession by a man or woman is itself grace.

Objectively, "Those who in themselves are disobedient are claimed and absorbed by the act of His obedience" (p. 693). They are obedient, yet they are exhorted to be obedient. "It is this very newness as such which has the significance and force of an imperative" (p. 694). But even in the Sermon on the Mount the imperative does not have the character of a general moral principle, as might appear in the case, for example, of 7:12a: "Whatsoever you wish that men would do to you, do so to them." This imperative has nothing whatever to do with "a recommendation to treat one's neighbour with an amiableness that one would like to receive from him" (p. 694). This Word is addressed by Jesus not to men and women in general but to his own, to those whom he called. His own are his witnesses, and what they can only wish is that others will approach them witnessing to his mercy and forgiveness, of which they ever stand in need, even as they are directed to approach others with the same witness. "They must not withhold from others the witness which they themselves need to receive from others" (p. 694).

Most pointedly the imperatives of the Sermon on the Mount direct those who have been given righteousness, sonship, and life in the kingdom not subjectively to cast away this gift, but rather to use it, to ever seek it. "That this asking, seeking and knocking are necessary, that the will of God, the life of grace, the righteousness of God's kingdom can be fulfilled only when this asking, seeking and knocking continually take place, is a clear reminder . . . that he who is called to follow Jesus is always as much in need of the Master Himself and His accomplished fulfillment of the Law (5:17) as he was on the first day — which means that apart from his relationship to Jesus . . . he would be no more than the Pharisees on the one hand and the heathen and publicans on the other" (p. 696).

In his summary, Barth concludes that the Sermon on the Mount is parallel to the Ten Commandments as a description of the conditions of life of the people of God, but is distinguished from the Decalogue inasmuch as the Sermon on the Mount describes the kingdom of God into which God has effectively translated men and women in the person of his Son (p. 697). This event, the coming of Jesus the Son of God, is reflected in the claims of the Sermon on the Mount and is what gives them their radical depth and true force. Those for whom Jesus came are to live from and for the grace and mercy of this coming — and not from or for anything else. Every difference between the requirements of the Ten Commandments and the Sermon on the Mount are a reflection of this point.

While the Sermon on the Mount directs Jesus' own to live from his grace and mercy, it does not replace "the events in which the life of God's people actually takes its course. . . . The individual concrete directions of Jesus to the men who surrounded Him . . . are no more made superfluous by the Sermon on the Mount than are the voice and leading of the angel by the Ten Commandments" (cf. Exod. 23:20ff.; p. 698). Of course the Sermon on the Mount delimits the sphere in which life in relationship with Jesus is lived, but the delimitation is not the living of that life — only its framework. Jesus will claim his own with the sharpness and depth that the Sermon on the Mount indicates. His own will recognize his voice in the concrete commands he gives them by the fact that it will confirm the framework that he has provided. But how Jesus will in fact govern his own "will have to be inferred from other parts of the Old and New Testaments. . . . A man can be obedient to the Sermon on the Mount only in so far as he is ready and prepared for acts of the most specific obedience . . . as [Jesus] demands them from every man in his own hour and situation" (p. 699).

In sum, the Ten Commandments and the Sermon on the Mount are not a general law of God, but rather delineations of the sphere of the people of God in which Yahweh in the Old Testament and Jesus in the New Testament confront certain specific men with concrete, definite commands. As a summary of the Lord's concrete commands, the requirements of these frameworks are neither addressed to an indeterminate number of men nor are they concerned in general with possibilities of human conduct. They aim, rather, "at the individual and concrete things which God will command and forbid man in regard to his behaviour in the context of [his] relationship [to the history of the covenant of grace]" (p. 700). They prepare the way for a specific obedience that is always new. They disclose the character of God and the distinctive features of the person who is specifically commanded by God.

We can now turn to the question, How are the concrete commands of Jesus, in which he appoints, calls, and commissions his twelve apostles, the concrete commands in which he gathers, upholds, and sends the men and women of his community that come after the time of his earthly ministry, intercessory death, and exaltation? The question is delicate since these commands are neither general nor a fixed pattern or law. Barth puts the question this way: Having demonstrated "that in the Bible itself the divine command is always a concrete command," how is "the concrete divine commanding which we find in the Bible [to be] understood as a divine command which concerns us also" (pp. 700-701)? Barth first enunciates the assumption of his expository answer. The Old and New Testaments testify to us, their readers and hearers, that Yahweh and Jesus confronted the persons of biblical history in specific ways, commanding one thing and forbidding another. Yahweh and Jesus have entered into relations with very definite men in very definite times commanding very definite actions and attitudes. "Yet [the Bible] does not give us this testimony merely out of an interest in the facts or a desire to record them, but in the character of a witness before a court of justice, whose statement is made for the sake of our judgment . . . with a view to our own decision and reaction to what is said. . . . The Bible wills that we should be contemporaneous with . . . these [biblical] men in regard to the divine command, our hearing and understanding of it, and our situation as affected by it" (p. 701).

In the first two chapters I followed Barth's elucidation, in several expository sections of the *Church Dogmatics,* of the New Testament depiction of the appointment, calling, and commissioning of the apostles. Connecting that elucidation with what Barth says here following upon the assumption just recounted, we can discern more clearly Barth's account of the enclosing or inclusive character of the apostolate. Jesus appointed, called, and commissioned the Twelve in prospect of his appointing, calling, and commissioning all human beings. Thus, actually or virtually all human beings are members of the apostolate (p. 702).

> The Bible tells us with . . . definiteness that a man of any other description than this does not exist. . . . The real command of God has the same aspect [for those who come after the apostles] as it bears in the Bible as an event of commanding and forbidding, obey-

ing and disobeying, between . . . [the Lord and man]. . . . The good required by the command of [the Lord] is not a general and intrinsic good, as is presupposed in every moral scheme, but the good . . . which bears the name of Jesus Christ. . . . [And Jesus and] man do not confront each other in empty space, but in a given space-time situation. . . . And the good of the command which He addresses to man, by which He invites him to be a participant, bearer, object and witness of His work . . . cannot in any sense be separated from [this space-time situation]. (P. 703)

What Jesus Christ commands is always participation in the proclamation of his kingdom.

There can never be any formal question of the performance of something good in itself, but always the material one of the execution of a commission or partial commission in the service of this cause. [Obeying] the command . . . in Scripture, like Abraham, Moses or David, Peter or Paul, the centurion of Capernaum or the rich young man, we constantly experience one of those greater or lesser movements of hope or gratitude, of expectant or fulfilled joy, performing those ministries of the servant or child which are good because they are necessary as a vital act of the divine community in its members, as an expression of the true Israel and the true Church, and their fulfillment is part of the earthly existence of the divine people and their vocation, and therefore a divinely appointed task. (P. 703)

To be involved in this work comes only by divine appointment. This appointment and "this commission, and therefore what is required of each individual in a specific time and situation, whether it be great or small, can not be undertaken by anyone out of nowhere, nor can it be self-prescribed and self-appointed. . . . [The] Judge, who is alone competent in this matter, will Himself dispose and decide. . . . [A] man will be and actually is told what is good and what the Lord requires of him — and with absolute definiteness. . . . According to the witness of Scripture. . . . He will always require of him specific things" (pp. 703-4).

But the Bible not only tells us that the command is and will be specific, it also tells us *what* the Lord specifically demands. The work of Jesus Christ is at once the Word (here, command) of Jesus Christ. What he performed with and for the apostles (and therefore demanded of them), he performed with and for them in prospect of all others. And by way of the performance of the apostles, the Word (demand) they heard and attest to is the Word (demand) that reaches those who come after Jesus' earthly ministry, death, and exaltation. The power of the divine act — Jesus' coming, intercessory death, and exaltation — is demonstrated in the gathering, upholding, and sending of the apostles. But its power is not exhausted in this movement, although its definite shape is manifested in it. This power, first bestowed on the apostles, is the power by which many (or all) others are drawn into the apostolate, its form after the Twelve and before the consummation of this gathering being the community.[13]

Jesus' activity in its totality (which includes its identification with God's activity), taken together with its expectation in Israel's witness, is the Word and, therefore, the command of God. The depiction of this activity in the New Testament can be denominated under the headings of appointment, calling, and commissioning. The Word and command of God is borne to those who come after Jesus' coming to the apostles by the person and word of the apostles. *Person* is used here to denote that what they were made participant in — Jesus' mission — is what the hearers of their word are made participant in. The command of the Lord that reaches others following them is the command of their appointment, calling, and commissioning. But it is not because it is their word that it is the divine command to others. It is because Jesus had the power to appoint, call, and commission the Twelve that he has the power to appoint, call, and commission those who hear the apostles' account of their appointment, calling, and commissioning by making it the Word of his specific command to many (or all). It is Yahweh or Christ who issues commands — definite commands — and not the prophets or apostles (p. 705).

But the Lord does not issue his commands apart from the witness of the prophets and apostles. While there is no abstract authority of the Bible, there is also no abstract authority of the Lord (p. 706). Later men and women are not only called in analogy with the calling of the apostles, they are not only called to become contemporaneous with the apostles, they are not only exhorted to hear the divine command with the apostles, but Jesus retains the power he had in calling the apostles to call others by the way of the apostles' account of their calling. The

---

13. Before the Bible is in the church, the church (in the original form of the Twelve) is in the Bible. This point is scarcely unique to Barth, but rather is characteristic of all Christians who affirm *sola Scriptura*.

apostles' task becomes our[14] task. Their situation and time is not ours, but the command remains both the same and definite. It is historically concrete and singular. It is not that we should only act *like* Peter or the centurion at Capernaum, but again act as those concretely commanded by Jesus,

> allowing the command given them to be again, in our very different time and situation, the command given here and now to us, and therefore ranking ourselves with them, and in their divinely addressed person taking our place in the history of . . . [the community], accepting and fulfilling our mission, or partial mission, not as something new and special, but as the renewal and confirmation of the task laid upon them. We cannot aspire to get beyond the existence of . . . the Church of Jesus Christ, which then and there . . . derived from the fulfillment of the covenant of grace. The people of God in *all* its members and in the whole life of its members can only be this people — Abraham and Peter. It can only live out its own history in this unique history [of Israel] and its sequel [the Church] and, therefore recognize in the wholly concrete commands . . . once given to the people of God the . . . commands given to itself. (P. 706)

The commands given the apostles were not temporary; they are the commands that Jesus, in his power, issues to us. It is our responsibility to perceive them as Jesus' definite commands to us, "to allow ourselves to be addressed as those to whom [the command] was given then and there . . . [to] accept it as also meant for us" (p. 707). But, "however we react to it, we are confronted and claimed by [the divine command], which wholly embraces and accompanies our whole life not only in accordance but in and with the fact that this happened to biblical man, the original and proper witness to the person and work of God, His severity and mercy" (p. 708).

## Frei and Barth

Barth speaks of the presence of Jesus as follows: Jesus chooses men to participate actively and passively in his coming. This is the goal of his

---

14. We follow Barth's use of the first person plural here in place of the third person plural, because of his stress on it at this point.

coming, and it is first realized in the apostolate, subsequently in the church's inclusion in the apostolate, and finally in the inclusion of many (or all) in the apostolate. To be a member of the church means to share the appointment, calling, and commissioning of the apostles with them, to share with them what they received and to perform with them what they performed, howbeit in a different time and situation. But it is not enough to say of a Christian that he or she is enrolled in the apostles' school. For Jesus who had the power to call the apostles retains the power to call others, who come after them, by way of the apostles' calling.[15] The Christian is the pupil gathered, upheld, and sent by Jesus himself by way of the apostles' account of Jesus' coming and their own calling into it. That is why Jesus' relation or presence to "us" is and can be so definite.

Frei speaks of the presence of Jesus as follows: The Word (Scripture and expository preaching) and sacraments are the temporal and spatial bases of Christ's indirect presence now; the church is the public form of Christ's indirect presence now. He is careful to understand the church as existing in a providentially ordered history in which its identity is enacted in its interaction with the world at large. The church's relation to Christ, then, has a twofold character. On the one hand the Word attests Jesus Christ to it, an attestation which Christ confirms to the church as it *lives in the Word.* On the other hand, it is the Jesus Christ identified by the Word to which the providential history, in which the church lives, is ordered. Clues to Christ's presence to and in history may be inferred from the Word by those who, while living in history, also live in the Word.

What Frei does not specify in *The Identity of Jesus Christ* is how it is that the church and its members live in the Word. For that specification we must attend to what he writes in *The Eclipse of Biblical Narrative.*[16]

## Frei: Living in the Word

From Frei's account of Western Christian reading of the Bible before the eighteenth century we can gain a clue as to what the phrase "living in the Word" indicates.[17] Before the advent of historical-critical theory, exposi-

15. "Call" and "calling" in this sentence are a short form for "appointment, calling, and commissioning."

16. Hans W. Frei, *The Eclipse of Biblical Narrative* (New Haven and London, 1974).

17. *Eclipse,* chap. 1.

tion of Scripture relied in large measure on the axiom that the combining of the biblical narratives into one cumulative narrative, by way of making earlier narratives types or figures of later ones, rendered an account or depiction of the real world. This depiction "must in principle embrace the experience of any present age and reader. Not only was it possible for him, it was also his duty to fit himself into that world in which he was in any case a member, and he too did so in part by figural interpretation and in part of course by his mode of life. He was to see his disposition, his actions and passions, the shape of his own life as well as that of his era's events as figures of that storied world." By figuration one "made sense of the extra-biblical structure of human existence, and of one's own experience. . . . [Biblical interpretation's] direction was that of incorporating extra-biblical thought, experience and reality into the one real world detailed and made accessible by the biblical story."[18]

The Protestant Reformers, living before the advent of historical-critical theory, instantiate, according to Frei, the "realistic" reading of Scripture. For Calvin, Scripture

> rendered . . . reality itself to the reader, making . . . reality accessible to him through its narrative web. He could therefore both comprehend it and shape his life in accordance with it. . . . Through the coincidence or even identity between the world being depicted and its reality being rendered to the reader (always under the form of the depiction), the reader or hearer in turn becomes part of that depicted reality and thus has to take a personal or life stance toward it. For Calvin . . . the cumulative *pattern constituting the biblical narrative* (the identification of God's dealing with the world in the peculiar way depicted in the promise of the law and its fulfillment in the gospel) is the setting forth of the reality which simultaneously constitutes its effective rendering to the reader by the Spirit.[19]

There is a harmony of depiction, the reality depicted and the reader's appropriation of reality brought about by the Holy Spirit. The work of the Spirit is integral to the reading of the biblical text, for the Spirit renders to the reader the reality depicted in the text engaging him with that reality.

Calvin employs typological or figural interpretation of the Bible in order to shape into one story the whole set of independent biblical stories. "In the service of the one temporally sequential reality the

18. *Eclipse,* p. 3.
19. *Eclipse,* p. 24.

stories become figures one of another without losing their independent or self-contained status."[20] Calvin reads each biblical story as literally descriptive, but the stories are coherent with one another and form one cumulative story by way of the stories being read as types of one another. "Figural interpretation, then, sets forth the unity of the canon as a single cumulative and complex pattern of meaning."[21] Literal reading sets forth the meaning of single stories; figural reading grasps the common pattern of the single stories and their meaning. It is not the case that the reader brings figural (or, for that matter, literal) meaning or interpretation to the text. Calvin is clear that, for example, the gift of the land of Canaan to the Israelites was a figure or type. The text of the Bible is always to be read forward, and not retrospectively, and that means that the figural pattern of meaning is integral to the Bible itself. Faithful interpretation is the comprehension of what is in the text and not a creation of the reader.

For Calvin, then, and this is Frei's own position, "we have reality only . . . under the narrative depiction which renders it, and not directly or without temporal narrative sequence . . . [and] we are, as interpreters as well as religious and moral persons, part of the same sequence. . . . The interpreter's situation is that of having to range himself into the same sequence by participating intellectually in it as a forward motion, a direction it still maintains."[22]

That is what Frei means by "living in the Word."

## Barth: Our Inclusion in the Apostolate

Earlier in this chapter I considered Barth's accounts of "our" being gathered by Christ and of the definiteness of Christ's presence to us now. In order to compare Frei's account of "living in the Word" with Barth's account of "our inclusion in the apostolate," we turn to some comments of Barth on the interpretation of Scripture in *C.D.* IV/3 and *C.D.* I/2. Although "living in the Word" and "our inclusion in the apostolate" suggest a degree of similarity between Frei and Barth, the difference in language here will redound in differences about the procedures of biblical interpretation, which I shall examine in the next chapter.

20. *Eclipse*, p. 28.
21. *Eclipse*, p. 33.
22. *Eclipse*, p. 36.

In the first text (*C.D.* IV/3, pp. 683-84) Barth makes no distinction between the apostolate and the church. They coincide. He observes that no passage in the Gospels directly refers to Jesus founding the church. Nor did the community that lives by the Gospels find any lacuna at this point. Why is this the case? Are we to suppose that there is no direct connection between the Jesus depicted in the Gospels and the existence of the community? Does Jesus' proclamation of the kingdom of God have nothing to do with the coming into existence of the church? Are the story of Jesus and the growth of the church quite distinct? Here is a classical instance of not seeing the wood for the trees. "The reason why the establishment of the community by Jesus Himself could not emerge as a definite and distinctive event in the Gospel account is rather that this is the theme of the whole Gospel narrative . . . the whole Gospel narrative as an account of Jesus necessarily [is] an account of the birth of the Christian community, of the development, corresponding to and consummating the unification of the twelve tribes of Israel in the Exodus from Egypt, of the people of God of the last time which has been inaugurated with the coming of Jesus Christ" (p. 683). One can, of course, point to distinct aspects of the birth of the community: the appointment of the Twelve, the mission of the Twelve, the words to Peter in Matthew 16:17ff., the beatitudes at the beginning of the Sermon on the Mount, the institution of the Lord's Supper, the feet washing, and the Great Commission. All of these texts bespeak aspects of the origin of the Christian community and of its origin in the will of Jesus and in his calling. But Barth's emphasis falls on the point that "the whole Gospel record at least from the baptism of Jesus in the Jordan to the story of Pentecost is implicitly also an account of the origin of this people, of its beginning in the words and acts of Jesus, of its gathering, maintaining, upbuilding, ordering and sending by Him" (p. 684). The "oldest history" of the community is found in the history of Jesus himself as depicted in the Gospels, so that by no means can we think to make the history of Jesus and the history of the community distinct. "Everywhere . . . the texts themselves speak of a Jesus who founds His community and of the community founded by Him" (p. 684).

Barth does not say anything different about the oneness of the apostolate and the church in his discussion of the interpretation of Scripture in *C.D.* I/2, portions of which I will now consider, but he qualifies the understanding of that oneness. The church, which includes many men and women actually and all men and women prospectively, can speak of its relationship with Jesus Christ only because of the existence of certain specific men. "The existence of these specific men [the apostles] is the existence of Jesus Christ for us [in the community actually] and for all men [in the community prospectively]" (p. 486). While the Christian community coincides with the apostolate, it coincides with it by virtue of its being included in it. The apostolate and the church are one by virtue of the former being the unvarying form of the latter. Or, more precisely, Jesus' relationship with the apostles and the apostles' relationship with Christ is the unvarying form of the church. In this the apostles are distinguished from church members who come after them, whom they resemble in all else (p. 486).

Barth develops further this differentiation of apostle and church member within the oneness of their community.

> [The apostles] are the first, who not only initiated the series [with those who come later] as a whole, but who must initiate afresh each individual link in it if it is properly to belong to the series. . . . There is, therefore, no direct connection of the church with Jesus Christ and no direct life by the Spirit — or rather the direct connection of the church with Jesus Christ and its direct life by His Spirit is that it should build on the foundation which He Himself laid by the appointment and calling of His [apostles]. . . . Without them there would be no church. Their existence is the concrete form of the [appointment and calling] of Jesus Christ Himself [which comes to church members and] in which the church has the foundation of its being. (P. 580)

The relationship of the apostles with their Lord is unique — as unique as Jesus' coming. "In the directness of their encounter with Jesus Christ, it is impossible for the disciples of Jesus to have real successors" (p. 671). It is to them that Jesus says, "You shall be my witnesses" and "Lo, I am with you always." These promises constitute the freedom of the apostles in two directions. In their freedom the apostles are copies of Jesus' own freedom and at the same time they are prototypes attesting the freedom of the members of the church (p. 671). It was Christ who freed the apostles to share in his mission. By way of their execution of their mission, Christ frees men and women now to share in his mission; it is only that they must receive him now by receiving the apostles. In the freedom of the apostles, "the Church must recognize and honour the freedom of their Lord in which the freedom of its members . . . is grounded" (p. 671). This means that the church is to "share in the movement in which Scripture was born. . . . Scripture does not spring only from obedience as such, but from the obedience of prophets and apostles discharged in this movement" (p. 671).

And finally Barth refers again to Peter and the confession he makes as depicted in Matthew 16:16-19. As the representative apostle, "he . . . becomes a subject distinct from both Jesus Christ and His Church, but mediating between them" (p. 673). In English the word *mediating* is too strong for this context.[23] Barth's point seems clearly to be that while Peter is a subject distinct from Jesus Christ and from the church, the church cannot know[24] Jesus Christ apart from Peter. The emphasis is upon the apostolate as the unvarying form of the church. The apostles knew the direct presence of Jesus in his activity of appointing, calling, and commissioning them. That is what gives the apostolate — in its movement of being gathered, upheld, and sent — its unique and ineffable and distinct character. Of course Peter is distinct from Christ — he is a disciple of Christ. But he is also distinct from later church members by virtue of his direct relationship with Christ, who directly fashioned him an apostle. In this sense Peter stands between Jesus and the later community. He is appointed by Jesus to stand "between" so that Jesus, by the Holy Spirit, can include in his relationship with Peter those who come later.[25] Indeed, Jesus gathered and upheld and sent Peter not only for Peter's sake, but for the sake of those who come after the time of Jesus' earthly ministry, death, and resurrection. It is this emphasis on mission and on the definite form of Christ's mission (and therefore on the definite form of his presence "to us" now) that is unattended by Frei and leads to differences in hermeneutical procedures between him and Barth. To these differences we shall now turn our attention.

---

23. Although it is hard to think what alternative for *vermittelndes* the translator had.

24. That is, *know* in the sense of know its relationship with Jesus, know Jesus' presence.

25. The differentiation in oneness is subtle.

# 4 Reading Scripture:
## A Comparison of Barth and Frei

A comparison of the ways in which Frei and Barth exposit Scripture must take as its content their respective expositions of the Gospel account of Jesus' passion, death, and resurrection, since that is the only portion of Scripture which Frei undertakes to exposit at any length. It will be necessary, then, to reintroduce, briefly, material from Frei's *Identity* already investigated in this study. However, in this chapter it will be examined strictly as a commentary on the Gospel episodes of the passion, death, and resurrection of Jesus.

## Barth's Commentary on the Passion and Death of Jesus (*C.D.* IV/2, pp. 250-64)

There is in the Gospel story a glaring contrast between, on the one hand, the beginning of Jesus' existence and his ministry in Galilee and, on the other hand, its end in Jerusalem. The Gospels signal this contrast with their depiction of the blindness of the disciples when Jesus spoke of his approaching death. "And taking the twelve aside, he said to them, 'Behold, we are going up to Jerusalem, and everything that is written of the Son of man by the prophets will be accomplished. For he will be delivered to the Gentiles, and will be mocked and shamefully treated and spit upon; they will scourge him and kill him, and on the third day he will rise.' But they understood none of these things; this saying was hid from them, and they did not grasp what was said" (Luke 18:31-34). In the parallel passage in Matthew's account, Jesus' prediction of his death is countered by Peter's rebuke, "God forbid, Lord! This shall never happen to you" (Matt. 16:22). And Luke recounts, even in the resurrection narrative, the traces of this rebuke, "we had hoped that he was the one to redeem Israel" (Luke 24:21). The darkness of Jesus' end, which the disciples could not penetrate, is a genuine darkness, for the Gospels are not afraid to depict Jesus himself wrestling with it in the Garden of Gethsemane and even in the cry of dereliction on the cross. But even as genuine darkness it does not break into Jesus' life as a catastrophe, according to the Gospel account, or even as an alien element in the sense that all that Jesus did he did in face of this element. "For all its glaring contrast, the story is seen [by the Synoptists] as a single whole" (p. 251). Death on the cross is the aim and goal of Jesus' existence, indeed its fulfillment. That is the secret made manifest in his resurrection.

The account of Jesus' prediction in Luke 9:43ff. is the one "in which the dumb astonishment of the disciples is most explicitly depicted" (p. 253). The narrative first depicts the disciples' wonder at all of the things that Jesus did;[1] next it recounts that Jesus said, "Let these words sink into your ears; for the Son of man is to be delivered into the hands of men"; and finally it goes on, "But they did not understand this saying, and it was concealed from them, that they should not perceive it; and they were afraid to ask him about this saying." The short passage that comprehends the ministry of Jesus, his passion and death, and, in the parallels, his resurrection, at once comprehends the disciples' response: first, their wonder at his sayings and works and, second, their confusion over his impending passion and death. That confusion shall extend into the period of the forty days and yet, then, their eyes shall be opened.

We observe in this exposition of Barth's how he, in seeking to follow the description of Jesus that the Gospels render, can only follow their description of what Jesus says and does and undergoes (with its contrasts and yet continuity) in terms of their account of what Jesus says and does and undergoes with and for the disciples and not at all in abstraction from his relationship with them. "It is integral to the passion story that it should be preceded by a particular demonstration of the Son of Man and the kingdom of God [to the disciples], and followed by the complete dumbfounding of the disciples" (p. 253). Does this order sug-

---

1. In Matt. 26:2 the introduction to Jesus' prediction makes reference to Jesus' sayings rather than to his deeds.

gest a "Yes, but"? There is, indeed, an anticlimax to Jesus' demonstration of the kingdom in the response of the disciples. But Jesus' death, as his prediction, is not an anticlimax to his demonstration of the kingdom. Rather, his death, following upon his demonstration of the kingdom, is the following of a "therefore" upon the "Yes." It is because the disciples do not understand the "therefore" that they do not understand the prediction, thus furnishing an anticlimax in the drama (p. 254).

The predictions do introduce a new element into the Gospel account. The end of the story is not self-evident. The confusion of the disciples serves to make that clear. For them the predictions are an anticlimax; Jesus is moving from the demonstration of the kingdom in word and act to an absurd future — a future in which the King will be delivered into the unclean hands of those who ought to worship at his feet; a future in which those who are disobedient to God triumph; a future in which the true and righteous benefactor suffers and dies as a criminal. "But what . . . the disciples did not see and hear then, they saw and heard . . . later — that what was predicted and then took place was not really a movement in an abnormal and crooked direction, but a movement from . . . the totality of the acts and words of Jesus to . . . the fulfilment of the kingdom of God inaugurated and revealed with His appearance" (p. 254).

Almost all of the predictions in the Synoptic Gospels, Barth observes, speak expressly of Jesus rising again on the third day. The emphasis of the predictions falls upon the death, but the reference to the resurrection in the predictions in the Synoptic Gospels indicates that the latter summon their readers to the forward movement of their accounts. If even from Jesus' death they look forward, then from the predictions themselves they look forward primarily to the prediction's fulfillment in Jesus' death (and to his death as the fulfillment of all of Jesus' sayings and deeds in demonstration of the kingdom). The movement to his death is, then, a forward movement and not an interruption, which is how the disciples initially perceived it.

Indeed, the death of Jesus as the genuine climax of his demonstration of the kingdom is indicated by the "must" present in the first instance of the prediction in all three of the Synoptics. "The Son of Man must suffer many things." Must Jesus suffer because of who he is, or in spite of who he is? Because of who he is — that is, in accord with his mission, in accord with the will of God for him. If possible, this emerges even more clearly in John, where in the words of Jesus his death is the forward reference that characterizes his life. "He is the Good

Shepherd who lays down His life for the sheep (10:11 and 15). He is the true Friend who lays down His life for His friends (15:13)" (p. 256).

For whom precisely does Jesus lay down his life? "For their sake I consecrate myself, that they also may be consecrated in truth. I do not pray for these only, but also for those who believe in me through their word" (John 17:19-20a). It is the disciples and those who believe in Jesus through their word who are consecrated by his death. While Barth's reading of the account of Jesus' passion and death, which account includes the predictions, leads him in his dogmatic formulations to speak of Jesus' death as the reconciliation of all flesh with God, he takes note in his expository section of this "striking passage" in John, in which Jesus is depicted as speaking of his death as his own consecration and, by way of it, that of his disciples and their believing hearers. We may understand Barth's reading to be that while all men and women are reconciled to God by Jesus' death, knowing participation in reconciliation is granted to the disciples and to many (all) others by way of the consecration of the disciples and of their hearers. Jesus consecrates himself by his fulfillment of God's mission for him and this fulfillment is what consecrates (*upholds* or *calls*) the disciples and with them all who believe in Jesus through their mission — prospectively all flesh.

Barth summons his readers to recognize in Paul's theology of the passion and death of Jesus the two themes that correspond to the depiction of Jesus' passion in the Synoptics. First, the aim of Jesus' life, indeed its fulfillment, is his death. Second, this fulfillment takes place, first of all, for the apostles. In relation to this second theme, Barth remarks, "For [Paul] knows that [Jesus] did not die in vain, but that He, the Son of God, 'loved me, and gave himself for me'" (Gal. 2:20). Paul says this in the context of his defense of his preaching and apostleship. Paul speaks more widely of Christ's death, for he declares that Jesus has "condemned sin in the flesh," the sin of the whole world (Rom. 8:3). Christ has put sin to death (Rom. 6:10). "Col. 1:9ff. is even more comprehensive, for it tells us that 'through the blood of His cross' He has created a cosmic peace which enfolds all things both in earth and heaven" (p. 257). But Paul can announce this cosmic reconciliation because Jesus' death is, in the order of knowing, in the first place that which upholds Paul, as he knows from his direct commissioning as an apostle by the risen Jesus, who was crucified. In relation to the first theme, Barth indicates that Paul could concentrate the significance of the historical existence of Jesus in his death, because the narration of

Jesus' life in the tradition was already a narration which found its climax in his death.

After an explication of Jesus' predictions in the Synoptics and a brief commentary on Paul's theology of Jesus' passion and death, Barth examines how the Gospels describe Jesus' life as directed toward his death. First, at his baptism "Jesus did not set Himself over others, but, in expectation of the imminent judgment of God, He set Himself in solidarity with them" (p. 258). To accept oneness with sinners is to accept God's imminent judgment and its execution upon himself. And not only in a passive way did Jesus accept this judgment. He appointed Judas to be an apostle. He did this knowing what Judas would do. "[Jesus] could hardly have integrated His self-offering more clearly into His life's work" (p. 259).

Second, Jesus in his intended action is never the sole agent depicted in the Gospels. He was delivered up by men, but also "by the determinate counsel and foreknowledge of God" (Acts 2:23). "God's providential rule was not contradicted by this event [of His death]" (p. 259). This "delivering up" by men, which God mysteriously merges into his providential ordering of events, is signalled throughout the account of his life; for example, by Herod's slaughter of the innocents (Matt. 2), the warning to Mary about the sword that would pierce her heart (Luke 2:35), the warning to the disciples that the Son of Man, like Elijah, will suffer at the hands of men (Matt. 17:12), the warning to the disciples that the night when no man can work will come (John 9:4; cf. John 13:30 where it does come with Judas' departure), and the warning to the disciples that the wicked husbandmen who have put to death the servants of their lord will destroy his beloved son (Mark 12:6ff.).

Third, it is Israel which delivered up Jesus, rejected him, and condemned him to death. "It is not for nothing that the one who initiates [the] action [against Jesus] is the apostle Judas, and in his person the elect tribe of Judah to which Christ Himself belonged, and in Judah . . . the chosen and called people of Israel" (p. 260). Jesus willed to gather Israel as his own, which in truth they were. "He came to His own but they received Him not" (John 1:11). "The whole history of Israel was repeated in concentrated form . . . : the presence of Yahweh to the one elect people" (p. 261). Israel's resistance to Jesus occurs throughout his life: it begins with the rejection of and attack upon Jesus in his hometown (Luke 4:22ff.), it continues with the rain of objections about the sabbath and fastings and purifyings, and mounts with the questions about Jesus' authority (Mark 11:28) and with attempts "to catch him in his words" (Mark 12:13ff.) and with the accusation that his power is of the devil. Mark speaks of a conference between Pharisees and Herodians about how to destroy him (3:6), John speaks of plots on his life (7:1, 25) and about the Council's hostility to him. Finally, all of the Synoptists speak of the taunts of the rulers at the foot of the cross.[2]

Fourth, if Jesus' life is directed toward his death, then we may expect to find this reflected in what the Gospels say about the disciples, for "a disciple is not above his teacher, nor a servant above his master; it is enough for the disciple to be like his teacher, and the servant like his master. If they have called the master of the house Beelzebul, how much more will they malign those of his household" (Matt. 10:24-25). Indeed, the existence of Jesus has a counterpart in the existence of the disciples. They will be "delivered up" to men (Matt. 10:17), reviled and persecuted and maligned for righteousness' sake (Matt. 10:5ff.). "They, too, will drink the cup that He drinks, and be baptized with the baptism He is baptized with (Mark 10:39)" (p. 264). "He who does not take his cross and follow me is not worthy of me," Jesus tells his disciples (Matt. 10:38). "There can be no question of identification with Him, of a repetition of His suffering and death. But it is a matter of [the disciples] . . . following 'in his steps'" (p. 264). "[This following] must not be equated or confused with the primary *theologia crucis*, which is wholly and exclusively that of the cross of Jesus, but it cannot and must not be separated from it" (p. 264).

## Barth's Commentary on the Resurrection and Ascension of Jesus (*C.D.* IV/2, pp. 131-54)

As in his exposition in *C.D.* IV/1, Barth in *C.D.* IV/2 observes that the gospel record is in three parts: the first part depicts Jesus' Galilean ministry and journey to Jerusalem, the second part depicts his passion, and the third short part describes his appearances to the apostles after his death. What is depicted in the third part is the decisive factor. Without this part the first two parts either would not have been composed or, if composed, composed in a very different way. And it is on the basis of the third part that the Lukan narrative can go on to speak

2. Barth concludes this section with the remark that the handing over of Jesus to the Gentiles by the Jews inaugurates the church as the community of Jews and Gentiles; that is, as the missionary community (p. 263).

of the outpouring of the Holy Spirit and its fruits in the Acts of the Apostles. It is to what happened in this part that the Epistles and Apocalypse look back — that is, to Jesus Christ as he appeared according to the concluding section of the gospel account. Everything said in Acts, the Epistles, and the Apocalypse is said on this basis. The community expects Jesus to come again in the mode in which he appeared to the apostles in the forty days. Jesus in this mode is its origin and goal. Likewise, everything said in the first two parts of the Gospels is said on this basis.[3] While the community is, of course, interested in his words and acts and crucifixion, it is interested in them because of who he is, and who he is is manifested to the apostles in the forty days and by way of the apostles' witness to many in the power of the Holy Spirit.

Jesus does not continue his existence in a changed form in the resurrection. Rather, the Jesus of the Galilean ministry and Jerusalem passion is manifested in his identity to the apostles in the forty days. How could the apostles have proclaimed Jesus in the fullness of his identity, when it was hidden from them "by the appearance of ignominy and despicability and insignificance" (p. 133)? The resurrection and ascension manifest Jesus' enacted identity as *the* Act and Word of God to his disciples. In his resurrection and ascension Jesus exercises his power to communicate himself, that is, who he is, effectively to the apostles and, by way of their mission, to many.[4]

> If the [disciples] of the New Testament could think and speak at all of Jesus Christ, if they had any right to do so, it was only as He had given Himself to be known as the One He was in His resurrection and ascension, as [He] was manifested to them in the revealing power of this event. . . . In His resurrection and ascension He gave Himself to be seen and heard and understood by them as the one He was and is. He became for them not only One who is but One who is also known. And what other ground could they possibly have for thinking and speaking of Him, for going out as His witnesses to Israel and to the Gentiles? As they did it on this ground, they did it as those who were authentically instructed, as those who

---

3. Barth doubts that there is any such thing as a genuine pre-Easter tradition.

4. There is a difference between the tendency of Barth's terminology and Frei's. Frei usually says "Jesus was manifested by the Father," while Barth tends to speak of "Jesus' self-manifestation." The difference is in tendency only, since Barth occasionally speaks of Jesus as manifested, and Frei speaks of Jesus as sharing his presence.

> genuinely knew Him, as witnesses of His history and existence
> whom He had authorized. (P. 134)

To say that the decisive factor in the gospel story occurs in the
third part of the narrative is not to diminish parts one and two. Rather,
part three tells of Jesus' manifestation to the apostles in such wise that
the first two parts are illumined by it and unified with it. For all their
novelty and particularity, the events of resurrection and ascension stand
side by side with the sequence of events that precede them. "But as
they stand side by side with this sequence, they illuminate and under-
line the new and peculiar features which . . . characterize this [whole]
sequence" (p. 135). A careful reading of the text will not allow a distinction to be made between the pre-Easter sequence and the post-
Easter sequence. The full sequence, illuminated by the narrative of the
forty days, is the completed act of God. The final act includes the first
two. But this is not merely a literary matter, as if reference is being made
only to the point that the redactors of the material shaped parts one
and two in the light of part three. Rather, Barth undertakes to demonstrate how in the Gospel account there is in the first two parts an
anticipation of the manifestation of Jesus to the apostles in his resurrection and ascension.

*Anticipation* indicates that the manifestation of the man Jesus, in
the mode of God, has not yet effectively occurred, yet objectively (and
not merely literarily) the earlier events in the sequence were also lights,
which in the event of the resurrection and ascension are coordinated
with and integrated into it. The disciples were with Jesus in his Galilean
ministry and Jerusalem passion, noticing, remembering, and registering
what was said and done, but not perceiving its true light. They were
witnesses, appointed and called, to what was said and done, but not
yet witnesses to what was said and done as the true light. They were
not yet committed to Jesus irrevocably. They did not yet know fully
who he was and is. In their reception of Jesus they did not yet offer
themselves as the rock on which he could build his church. Indeed,
Jesus himself exercises restraint in the first two periods, "not willing
that He should as yet be confessed or proclaimed" (p. 136). Yet in the
pre-Easter stage Jesus says to Peter that he is the rock on which he will
build his church (Matt. 16:18). And Peter does recognize and confess
the man Jesus as the Christ, the Son of the living God, and he does so
because it has been revealed to him by the Father who is in heaven.
The very isolation of this text in the pre-Easter stage instantiates the

fact that the disciples are not yet "alert, percipient and confessing witnesses" (p. 136), yet its presence anticipates their becoming such witnesses.

The secret of Jesus' identity is constantly broken by the miracles he performs in connection with his proclamation of the kingdom, yet their effectiveness as manifestations of his identity is qualified by his sometimes forbidding those who were witnesses and/or recipients of a miracle from speaking about it. The secret of Jesus' identity is broken by the children in the Temple who cry, "Hosanna to the Son of David" (Matt. 21:15ff.), and by the centurion who cries out, "Truly this was the Son of God" (Matt. 27:54), but Jesus in the Synoptics makes no self-witness to this effect. Yet we cannot say that no explicit declarations of his identity are made, for example, Jesus' "I am" in reply to the high priest's question, "Are you the Christ, the Son of the Blessed?" (Mark 14:61-62). And all of the Gospels describe Jesus as always surrounded by joyful and startled wonderers, yet, again, they are not bound to him.

Most clearly, the transfiguration is an anticipation of the resurrection. In all three accounts it follows Peter's confession, the first prediction of the passion (and resurrection), and the saying about what following Jesus means for the apostles. It is directly preceded by the announcement that some of those present would not die before they had seen the kingdom of God come in power and is directly followed by Jesus' healing of the epileptic boy, whom the disciples could not heal. The event itself has three elements. The first is the change in Jesus' form seen by Peter, James, and John. His face shone as the sun, his garments became exceeding white. The three disciples see Jesus as the Son of Man in his kingdom. The second is the appearance of Moses and Elijah, who, according to Luke, talk with Jesus about the exodus he will accomplish in Jerusalem (Luke 9:31). The third element is the cloud, which reveals and conceals the divine presence, from which a voice declares, "This is my beloved Son" and "Hear him." The appearance is distinguished from the resurrection appearances by the fact that Jesus enjoins the disciples not to speak of it, "until the Son of man should have risen from the dead" (Mark 9:9), making both what was seen and the seeing of it provisional.

The inability of the disciples to heal the epileptic boy bespeaks their continuing lack of power. The cry of the boy's father, "Lord I believe, help Thou my unbelief," characterizes the disciples as well. That characterization continues into the forty days and after, and is only overcome as the apostles are reached by the self-witness of Jesus in the resurrection. "Even so . . . it is plain that [the Gospel account] does ascribe to [the transfiguration], and to the whole pre-Easter history and existence [of Jesus] explicitly as it possibly can, the same quality as it later gives to their definitive actualization in the accounts of [Jesus'] resurrection and ascension" (p. 138).

What is remarkable in the Gospels is how "the earlier and later elements in the history of Jesus belonged together, how necessarily they lit up and interpreted each other" (pp. 138-39). The resurrection and ascension are so much the climactic point of the Gospel account that every event depicted in it, without any loss to its individual integrity, is an anticipation of this climax. In his ministry and passion Jesus enacts his identity, which is manifested in the forty days, but the events of his enactment anticipate at every point this manifestation. In John's Gospel the tension between Jesus' enactment of his identity and its manifestation is reduced to a minimum. "We might almost say that in the story of Jesus in the Fourth Gospel we have one long story of the transfiguration" (p. 139). Yet even in the Fourth Gospel, "There is no abolishing of the distinction between before and after" (p. 139), that is, between Jesus' enactment of his identity and its climactic manifestation, although often enough in John the anticipation of the manifestation might be understood more as a "very nearly" than as a "not yet." In the comparison of the Synoptics with John we may estimate that John emphasizes the continuity of the depiction of Jesus, before and after Easter, in his account, while the Synoptists emphasize the movement from the concealment of Jesus' identity to its manifestation.[5]

Following upon his discussion of the event of the resurrection and ascension as the climactic event of the sequence of events that comprise the gospel story (and as the decisive event that gives rise to the apostolic story), Barth turns to a discussion of the particular elements in the event of the resurrection and ascension. He begins with a question: Why is it only after his death that Jesus' identity is effectively manifested to the disciples? Why is it that even in John's Gospel this is the case? The first answer is simple, if basic, and because of its simplicity might be overlooked. Until Jesus' death on the cross he had not fully enacted his identity. Throughout the Gospel account he is enacting his identity, but how could he be manifested in the fullness of his identity

---

5. Barth refers here not to a simple progression, but to the point that the same Jesus is manifested differently to the disciples before the forty days and during the forty days.

until it was fully enacted? What more can the earlier stages of the Gospels be than anticipations of the manifestation of his full identity? The manifestation of Jesus in the resurrection and ascension is, then, distinguished from what is "manifested" of Jesus before his death not in degree, but in principle. The resurrection and ascension are the manifestation of Jesus in the fullness of his enacted identity.

But beyond the first and simple answer, it is necessary to attend, after all, to the contents of Jesus' identity. Jesus intended in his life, and enacted this intention in his sacrifice of it, to substitute himself in the place of guilty and condemned human beings, to receive on their behalf the death due them, to free them from God's sentence of condemnation for sin.[6] He intended and enacted this because it was God's will for him to do so; for this he was sent. It was only upon his substitution of his death for others' deaths that he could be manifested to these others in his identity as their Savior. It is, then, the material identity of Jesus, which he completes in his suffering on the cross, that answers the question about why the resurrection is *the* manifestation of Jesus. Jesus' history and existence are completed or fulfilled in his death on the cross, for there he suffered death in the place of all others, freeing all from death. His act is perfect in the sense that it need not and therefore cannot be continued, augmented, or superceded. Barth extends this statement about the sufficiency (perfection) of the event of Christ's death for the forgiveness of all sins to the sufficiency (perfection) of the resurrection and ascension of Jesus as the revelation or manifestation of this event and of the person of this event. As the event of Jesus' death is perfect, so, in the same sense of the word, is the manifestation of this event (and the person of this event) in the resurrection and ascension. This event will not be replaced by the final Parousia, which will still be the same manifestation, nor by the Holy Spirit.

> Wherever [Jesus] is . . . known, by the witness of the Holy Spirit, in the time between, the time of the community, it is always in the glory in which He was then manifested to the disciples and known by them. His completed [identity] and work, and its completed revelation, were sufficient then, and they are sufficient today, and they will be sufficient for all times, and even when time shall be no more. The resurrection and ascension are this once for all and all-

6. He does this for all human beings, even as he does this, in the first place, for the apostles and, then, for Israel.

> sufficient event of revelation . . . the event in which the basis of the
> knowledge of Christ which we seek was and is laid. This is the
> objective basis from which alone, by the witness of the Holy Spirit,
> all subjective knowledge of Jesus Christ can derive — the knowl-
> edge of the disciples, the first community and the later Church.
> (P. 142)

While the resurrection-ascension is the revelation of the event of
Jesus' death (the death comprehending his life as its aim), as this revelation it is itself an event. It takes place after Jesus' death as another
event in Jesus' existence, and like the event of Jesus' death takes place
in the world of time and space.

> It, too, was experienced and attested, not only inwardly but out-
> wardly, by certain men. . . . It is an event which involves a definite
> seeing with the eyes and hearing with the ears and handling with
> the hands, as the Easter stories say so unmistakably and emphati-
> cally. . . . In spite of the extraordinary nature of what happens, the
> reaction of the disciples is a normal reaction according to the unan-
> imous testimony of the accounts. In its good points and not so good
> it is quite in keeping with all that we have been told concerning
> them. . . . [It is to be noted that] apart from the existing circle of the
> disciples there are no witnesses at all of the event. (P. 143)[7]

If it were not an event in the world of space and time, "it would not
be an event of revelation. The fact that it was an event of this kind, and
had a decisive significance as such, emerges afterwards in the changed
attitude of the disciples to their Lord. . . . [As] an event of this kind, it
was a concrete element in [the disciples'] history, and therefore a concrete event in history at large" (p. 143).

The Gospels, in the third stage, depict the event as a series of
encounters and brief conversations between Jesus and his disciples. The
execution and termination of these encounters is always in Jesus' hands,
not in the hands of the disciples. The disciples do not seek or find or
even expect Jesus. "Jesus came" (John 20:24, 26). "Jesus himself drew
near and went with them" (Luke 24:15). "Jesus met them" (Matt. 28:9).
Jesus stood in the midst of his disciples (Luke 24:36). "It is never ex-

7. "Disciples" is used here in the wider sense, which includes the women
and the Twelve and the five hundred of 1 Cor. 15:5ff. Paul, as Barth notes, is the
great exception to the rule, for in his case the risen Jesus appeared to an "unbeliever."

plained where He came from, or how He came" (p. 144). We read in John 21:14, "Jesus was manifested (ἐφανερώθη) to his disciples" and, according to Barth, this is to be read in light of John 21:1, "Jesus manifested himself again to the disciples." This is a piece with the ὤφθη ("he appeared") of 1 Corinthians 15:5ff. The eleven disciples "saw him" (Matt. 28:16-17). "But . . . this perception is not as simple as all that. He can be perceived only as He comes. And whether or not they see Him effectively is not under their control" (p. 144). "God raised Jesus on the third day and made him manifest . . . to us who were chosen by God as witnesses" (Acts 10:40-41). Jesus is seen and heard on the Emmaus road by his disciples, but not at first recognized. "Their eyes were kept from recognizing him" (Luke 24:16). And even when the disciples see and hear they doubt (Matt. 28:16). When they see and hear and believe, this "possibility and freedom . . . always seem to be given them by Jesus Himself. . . . There is no longer any question of a continuous companionship of Jesus with His disciples, but always of individual encounters with them which He Himself both began and terminated" (p. 144). The ascension terminates one of these encounters and the whole event.

The meaning of the encounters, not separable from the narrated sequence as such, is that Jesus now manifested himself to the disciples in the fullness of his enacted identity, that identity which he had begun to enact in his ministry and conclusively enacted by his reception of suffering and death. And the disciples now received Jesus' effective manifestation of his identity, the enactment of which they had already witnessed but not perceived. Why did they now perceive it? Surely not because of a new and glorified corporeality. We find more about a new and glorified corporeality in the account of the transfiguration than in the resurrection-ascension narrative. "What the Evangelists really know and say is simply that the disciples saw and heard Jesus again after His death, and that as they saw and heard Him they recognized Him, and that they recognized Him on the basis of His identity with the One whom they had known before" (p. 145). The disciples who went to Emmaus say that he was known to them "in the breaking of the bread" (Luke 24:35), in the action in which they had known him at the Last Supper and at the feeding of the five and four thousand. And the accounts of the touching of him (Luke 24:39; John 20:20, 25, 27) indicate that he gives himself to be known to the disciples as the One they knew as crucified. How is it that when Jesus came to the disciples by the Sea of Tiberias they recognized him? Again the common meal in which Jesus is host plays a part.

> But surely the simplest explanation of their recognition is that the whole incident is an unmistakeable reflection . . . of Peter's great draught of fishes in Luke 5:4-11. . . . It is Peter who plunges out of the ship to reach Him in the quickest possible way — the same Peter who had once done something like this before (Matt. 14:19), but who above all had been told in Luke 10:15, 'Do not be afraid; henceforth you shall catch men.' . . . [The closing of the account of this incident in John] has as its theme the sending . . . of Peter (21:15-23). . . . If we can . . . understand the missionary command of Matt. 28:18ff. as a forceful extension and yet also a confirmation of the commission of Matt. 10:5-42, the question how the doubts of the disciples in Matt. 28:17 were overcome is readily answered. . . . [The meaning and effectiveness] of the self manifestation of the risen Christ is to be found always in the demonstration of His identity with the One who had lived and taught and acted and gone to His death. (P. 145)

It is not only by his resurrection that Jesus gains his identity. He became who he was and is in his life and death — the Savior. "The point about His resurrection is that in it He reveals Himself as the One who was and is and will be this in His life and death" (p. 145). *In nuce*, what Jesus was for the disciples, he, in his resurrection, manifests he is and always will be for them. Yet, since he sends them to the end of the earth, not for them only, but for all, he is and always will be what he was for them.

The event of the resurrection is the concrete event of Jesus' self-manifestation after his death to the apostles (and by way of their word to all). He is with them in his fully enacted identity, as Savior. The resurrection is the event in which he makes it possible for the disciples to perceive that he still is and who he is. Jesus Christ is and can now be known and loved in this world of time and space. The truth of who he is and what he has done is imparted to the human beings, in the first place the disciples, for whom he came and acted.

But it is critical, Barth argues, to recognize a limitation to Jesus' self-impartation. Since the truth of who he is and what he has done is imparted to men by Jesus' demonstration to them that "He still is" (the One he was), his self-manifestation occurs by the act of God. The New Testament tells us "decisively that the event of Easter has to be understood . . . as the raising which happens to Jesus Christ. . . . Certainly in the resurrection of Jesus Christ we have to do with a movement and action . . . in which Jesus Christ as the Son of God has . . . [a part] . . .

yet only as a pure object and recipient of the grace of God [the Father]."[8]
The very event in which Jesus manifests his identity to certain men, so
they may know and love and depend upon him, has the incomprehensible character that belongs to the act of God.[9] If the apostles, and men
and women after them by way of their word, have a knowledge of
Jesus' identity, it is because Jesus, in the power of God's act, shares it
with them. This means that they can neither gain it from themselves
nor at any time exercise any control over it. They cannot make it comprehensible to themselves or others, but must rely on him "who still is
and shall be forevermore" in the power of God's act to make it comprehensible to them. Knowledge of Jesus' resurrection, then,

> is bound always to Him and conditioned by Him . . . [and, therefore]
> it will include an acknowledgement of the inexplicable and incon-
> ceivable nature of its occurrence [as God's act]. Because the One
> who is revealed in it is the living Jesus Christ, He will as such be
> an object and content which cannot be exhausted in any dimension.
> [But] because it is an event which took place for the apostles in their
> encounter with the living Christ, the knowledge of it will necessarily
> be ordered by their witness and continually be orientated by it. And
> . . . because that which is revealed in it is [His] . . . saving act for
> us, a genuine and fruitful knowledge of it will necessarily become
> and be the knowledge of our love for the One who has first loved
> us in Jesus Christ. (P. 149)

While the knowledge of Jesus' resurrection depends upon the
living Jesus Christ sharing himself in it with (first the apostles and then)
us, and will be the knowledge of our love for him and the One who
sent him, it is yet "historical knowledge" in two senses, which Barth
elucidates. First, our knowledge of it "will involve the most impartial
and painstaking investigation of the *texts* which speak of this event"
(p. 149). Such an investigation will not seek some alleged "historical
facts" behind the texts, but rather will investigate the historical texts
themselves. Second, the investigation will be *impartial*. It will seek to
find what the texts say in their attestation of this event. It will not fit
them into some picture of the world and history. It will not prescribe
in advance what the texts can and cannot say, nor will it impose questions on the texts that the texts themselves do not ask, but rather will

8. *C.D.* IV/1, pp. 303-4.
9. "They were afraid" (Mark 16:8); cf. Luke 24:37.

attend to the questions that the texts raise and remain open to the replies that they give. It belongs to this impartiality that "we allow the New Testament texts to say what they themselves wish to say and do actually say" (p. 150).

Barth, as has become evident, speaks of the resurrection and ascension as one event. The resurrection is the *terminus a quo*, the ascension the *terminus ad quem* of this event. "Between the two there take place the appearances of Jesus Christ which are the proper theme of the New Testament narrative" (p. 150). In relation to the resurrection as the *terminus a quo* of this event Barth poses the question: "Where did Jesus come from?" The Gospel account gives two replies. First, he came from death, the death of a condemned criminal. He came from burial, from being "removed from the sight of the living, delivered up to the long but accelerating process of being forgotten. He had gone to the place where all men must go . . . but from which none can ever return. And it was from this place that He did in fact return. . . . He now had behind Him that which can only be in front of all other men" (pp. 151-52).

Second, the Easter narratives attest that Jesus arose from *the dead*.

> From the innumerable host of the dead this one man, who was the Son of God, was summoned and awakened and reconstituted as a living man, the same man as He had been before. . . . It is in consequence of this that He appears to His disciples. It is with this that there commences His revelation as the One He was before. . . . He had already been present to His disciples (and all the people) as this man. He had already spoken to them as such, and called them and sent them and done signs and wonders. He had concealed Himself from them as such, but not totally. . . . They had already recognized Him as such, but not properly. . . . [However, in what] the Baptist had already seen and declared [namely, that He was] . . . the Lamb of God which takes away the sin of the world . . . He was wrapped in total concealment, and not at all known by [the disciples]. . . . [Now] as such He was revealed [to them] . . . as the One who came from this event [of arising from the dead]. (P. 152)

He comes not only from death, but from the resurrection from the dead. "It was in the man who came visibly and audibly and perceptibly . . . from His death . . . His tomb . . . but also from His resurrection from the dead, in His coming from the place from which none other has ever come, that they knew Him as the One He was and is . . . the Lord" (pp. 152-53).

The ascension of Jesus is the *terminus ad quem* of the forty days. Barth poses the question, "Where did Jesus go?" and again finds two answers in the Gospel account. The first reply, given by Luke in 24:51 and Acts 1:9-11, is "to heaven," that is, to a place inaccessible to human beings. But the second reply is the decisive one. He went to God.

> In biblical terminology heaven is the dwelling place of God . . . the place of His throne . . . from which he rules and speaks and acts . . . from which He blesses and judges the earth and man, from which He causes His will to be done on earth, His Kingdom . . . to come on earth. . . . And the 'cloud' which parted Jesus from the eyes [of the disciples] in Acts 1:9 . . . is nothing other than the aureole of [this] . . . sphere of the divine dominion, the dwelling of the Father as it becomes visibly present on earth. . . . The disciples saw the man Jesus received into this 'cloud'. That this is the decisive element in the conclusion of the Easter story emerges clearly from the New Testament statements in which the resurrection is brought into direct connection with the session at the right hand of God (Rom. 1:4, 8:34; Col. 1:3; I Peter 3:22; Eph. 1:20, etc.). (Pp. 153-54)

What is revealed in the event of the ascension is that God rules in fellowship with this man who comes from death and from his awakening from the dead, and this man rules in his fellowship with God. "The risen Jesus declared Himself to his disciples as the One who went to this place, and He was known to them as such, and therefore as the One He was and is. In His going to this place He was known as the Lord, in the unlimited power of the concept. . . . This is why, in view of His going to this place, the disciples could look ahead to their own future and that of the world, awaiting the witness of the Holy Spirit from heaven, and awaiting finally the coming again of the same Lord from heaven" (p. 154).

## Frei's Commentary on the Passion and Death of Jesus

Only a brief account of Frei's commentary on the passion and death of Jesus need be rendered, since this material has already been introduced. In any case, a concise résumé will be sufficient to serve the intention of comparing Frei's exposition with Barth's with a view to elucidating aspects of their respective interpretive procedures.

We begin with Frei's summary of the "patterns of meaning" that he observes as present in the account of Jesus' passion and death. (1) Jesus' willing reception of his passion and death is the enactment of his intention to obey God. Jesus' obedience to God is the first pattern of meaning embedded in the passion-death sequence of events in the gospel story.[10] (2) In the passion and death sequence Jesus retains power and yet is at once powerless. It would be difficult to deny power to Jesus in his passion and death, since "it is his vicarious identification with the guilty and, at the climax of the story, his identification with the helplessness of the guilty that provides the Gospel's story of salvation" (p. 104). (3) Yet Jesus genuinely becomes powerless, for "he cannot save himself" (Mark 15:31). There is a genuine transition from power to powerlessness which obtains simultaneously with the coexistence of power and powerlessness in Jesus' activity and willed passivity. (4) "The exact circumstances climaxing [Jesus'] story were not completely initiated and executed at his behest. On the other hand, he did not passively await and accept them. In fact, his identity is revealed in the mysterious unity of his own decision and determination with the circumstances and events of his passion and death" (p. 105). The gospel story does not depict these circumstances and events as "fated," but rather the coincidence of Jesus' enacted intention with the train of circumstances in the narrative sequence is recounted as the interrelation of Jesus' and the Father's intention and action. We can now, still briefly, observe Frei's development of his account of each of these patterns of meaning.

(1) All four Gospels stress the motif of Jesus' obedience. "As a storied figure, it is . . . his mission and his obedience to it to which constant reference is made. He is one who is 'sent'" (p. 106). Jesus' reference to his mission appears in all of the Gospels and is, of course, a reference to his relationship with the One who sent him. To this point Frei quickly returns. But before he does, he interjects an important point. The emphasis on mission indicates that the center of Jesus' person is not within himself, but rather to be found "in relation to the events of his life and the persons with whom he came in contact" (p. 107). While there is little reference in Frei's exposition to Jesus' being sent to the apostles or to the apostles' inclusion in his mission, Frei acknowledges that Jesus' identity is enacted in his relation to others, even if the "others" are not specified nor spoken of as "unsubstitutable."

---

10. "The resurrection demonstrates Jesus' acceptability to God as being obedient to God's will" (p. 103).

But for Frei, who quickly returns to this, the critical point of Jesus' repeated reference to his mission is that his identity is enacted in relation to the Father who sent him and to whom he is obedient. "Jesus' very identity involves the will and purpose of the Father who sent him. He becomes who he is in the story by consenting to God's intention and by enacting that intention in the midst of the circumstances that devolve around him as the fulfilment of God's purpose" (p. 107). Jesus' specific being is in specific actions centered on his obedience moving toward a specific goal. This gives a clue to how others are to see their own identity in relation to Jesus, that is, in obedience.[11] It is in obedience to God that Jesus holds together in his person the coexistence of his power and powerlessness and his transition from power to powerlessness.

(2) In the third stage of the gospel story is an unbroken sequence of events. In this sequence the account of Jesus in the Garden of Gethsemane "marks the crucial *inner* transition point from power and scope to powerlessness" (p. 109). The stress is upon Jesus' determination to be obedient. "Corresponding to [this] transition from power to helplessness on the inner plane is its constituting enactment on the *outer* plane" (p. 110). The enactment is what is narrated from this point to the end of the Gospel account. Jesus' words at his arrest signal the movement from the inner to the outer plane. "Do you think I cannot appeal to my Father, and he will at once send me more than twelve legions of angels? But how then should the scriptures be fulfilled, that it must be so?" (Matt. 26:53-54). Jesus both initiates and consents to the coming shape of events in his obedience to God.

The first pattern of meaning Frei describes by the rubric, "Jesus was obedient." The second pattern of meaning elucidates the content of Jesus' obedience. It does so in terms of the pattern of exchange drawn from Deutero-Isaiah. "The Son of man came not to be served but to serve, and to give his life as a ransom for many" (Matt. 20:28); "he poured out his soul to death, and was numbered with the transgressors; yet he bore the sin of many, and made intercession for the transgressors" (Isa. 53:12). "To be obedient to God was to pour out his blood in behalf of men" (p. 111). The coexistence of power and powerlessness is evident. Jesus' power resides in his bearing and therein bearing away the sin of many; his powerlessness resides in the fact that he cannot save himself from

---

11. Barth would add: not in any obedience, but rather in the concretely shaped obedience of the apostles to their appointment, calling, and commissioning.

death, but must be subjected to it. His power for others lies in his powerlessness to save himself. This coexistence of power and powerlessness is described at several places in the third stage of the Gospel narrative. Most pointedly, we read in Mark 15:31, "He saved others, he cannot save himself"; as he stands as the accused before the Roman governor, Jesus turns the governor's question, "Are you the King of the Jews?" into an unwitting testimony to him as the Christ; and upon the cross he promises the thief that he shall be with him in paradise. In John's Gospel (10:17-18), Jesus is depicted as saying, almost to the point of the elimination of his powerlessness, "I lay down my own life. . . . No one takes it from me, but I lay it down of my own accord."[12]

(3) While the Synoptists attest the coexistence of the power and powerlessness of Jesus, they nevertheless depict a genuine transition from power to powerlessness. Again, Frei reminds his reader that these terms are not abstract, but rather describe Jesus moving from a certain liberty of action to a certain elimination of it. "The transition is effected through [Jesus'] own decision, as well as through the action of the authorities" (p. 113). And it is irreversible. Once Jesus gives himself into the hands of the authorities, his liberty of action comes to an end and he will almost certainly be put to death. After the scene in the Garden of Gethsemane we are not unprepared for what follows. In each succeeding event Jesus' liberty is increasingly constricted. With his death, all liberty of action is eliminated. Jesus intended to obey the will of God. He enacted his intention and obeyed the will of God in relinquishing power and accepting powerlessness — genuine powerlessness. "The pattern of significance embedded in this intention-action sequence is startling illumined by the words of Jesus near the beginning ('Yet not what I will, but what Thou wilt') and by the rulers' words at its consummation ('He saved others, he cannot save himself'). In these two sayings and in the events they circumscribe, we see the transition of Jesus from power to powerlessness" (p. 115).

(4) The fourth pattern of meaning to be observed, now in relation to, rather than embedded in, the account of Jesus' passion and death, is the interrelation of the Father's and Jesus' intention and action. This pattern is embedded in the narrative about Jesus risen from the dead. So we turn to Frei's commentary on the account of Jesus' resurrection.

---

12. Frei finds the pattern of the coexistence of power and powerlessness a complex and critical pattern embedded in the Synoptics, but finds it very nearly eliminated in the Fourth Gospel.

## Frei's Commentary on the Resurrection of Jesus

Once Jesus consents to initiative passing from his hands, to whom does it pass? The immediate answer is "to historical forces," that is, to his accusers and judges, to the interests they represent, and behind them to "a vast mass of humanity." But, mysteriously, at their common point of impact — Jesus' judgment and death — the power of God and that of the historical forces coincide. This "mergence" may be observed in all of the Gospels. It is plainly expressed in John's Gospel, where Pilate says to Jesus, "Do you not know that I have the power to release you, and the power to crucify you?" Jesus replies, "You would have no power over me unless it had been given you from above" (John 19:10-11). "It is at this point that Pilate's power and the power of God cohere" (p. 117). The initiative of the historical forces and God cohere at this point and seem to increase in proportion to the decrease of initiative on Jesus' part.

Yet there is a critical limitation to this observation. Even as God's initiative, which governs the actions of Jesus' opponents, supercedes the initiative of Jesus, God's intentions and actions and those of Jesus are increasingly identified. Even so, Jesus and God are not merged. Jesus retains his identity. "What emerges is a motif of supplantation and yet identification" (p. 118). This pattern is deeply embedded in the Synoptic Gospels. The dominance of God's activity over Jesus' activity that begins with the scene in the Garden of Gethsemane reaches its climax in the account of Jesus' resurrection. Jesus from Gethsemane forward is increasingly passive. Finally, he is dead and buried. No activity is possible for him. In the resurrection *God*, and God alone, is active — directly and exclusively. Yet *Jesus,* and Jesus alone, appears, the same Jesus who enacted his identity in his obedience to God. In the resurrection narratives "God" is scarcely mentioned (although Acts and the Epistles make clear that "God" raised Jesus from the dead). "The absolute and direct initiative of God, reaching its climax at this point and stressed in the early preaching of the church, is completely unmentioned in the narrative itself" (p. 121). Frei makes this summary observation: "In his passion and death the initiative of Jesus disappears more and more into that of God; but in the resurrection, where the initiative of God is finally and decisively climaxed and he alone is and can be active, the sole identity to mark the presence of that activity is Jesus. God remains hidden, and even reference to him is almost altogether lacking. Jesus of Nazareth, he and none other, marks the presence of the action of God" (p. 121).

Frei, having made the critical point about Jesus' resurrection in observing that here where God, and God alone, acts, Jesus, and Jesus alone, appears, next carefully examines the elements in the narrative in order to take into account the complexity of the relation between Jesus and God. In the final sequence of the Gospel narrative, Jesus is in need of redemption and is, in fact, redeemed. "The resurrection is the vindication in act of [Jesus'] own intention and God's. [But particular attention should be accorded the point that] in the unity and transition between his need of redemption and his being in fact redeemed, Jesus' identity is focused, and *the complex relation and distinction between his identity and that of God is manifested*" (p. 121, italics added). While there is a real transition from Jesus' need of redemption to the fact of his redemption, their unity rests in Jesus' subject self — the same Jesus is crucified and raised. And this unity in transition focuses Jesus' identity, which means that the crucifixion remains a part of the identity of Jesus raised from the dead. That is scarcely a startling claim. But it is more startling when reiterated in terms of the claim that Jesus holds power and powerlessness together, for then it is said that Jesus "holds together his own identity in the transition from death to resurrection" (p. 122). Is that to say that Jesus enacts his own resurrection? "Since Jesus enacted his identity in what he did and underwent, and since his identity is the same — that of Jesus of Nazareth — in crucifixion and resurrection, does the story suggest that he raised himself from the dead?" (p. 123). The New Testament does not speak in this way.

Thus, in order to follow the Gospel narratives into the concluding portion of stage three, into the *narrative* that is the climactic summation of all of the preceding narratives, a simple application of the intention-action and self-manifestation schemata to the material is inadequate. That is because there is neither a simple unification of Jesus and God nor a simple distinction. And this prompts an intermingling of the schemata. Jesus is set forth in his resurrection as the manifestation of God's action. The correlate for *action* in the simple application of the first schema is *enactment in public occurrence*, and the correlate for *manifestation* in the simple application of the second schema is *self*. Yet the resurrection is set forth in the gospel story as the *manifestation* of God's *action*. Moreover, God's deed is an *action* in which Jesus is *manifested*. Here, where elucidation of the narrative demands an intermingling of the schemata, the pattern of unification between Jesus and God prevails: God acts, Jesus appears. "Yet this particular emphasis meets a firm limit because the logic of the story and of the situation . . . suggest that the resurrection of Jesus as an *enacted event*, and not merely

as the *manifestation* of his *identity,* is the climax of the Gospel narrative"
(p. 124). While an intermingling of the two schemata is necessary in
order to elucidate the final portion of the Gospel narrative, the schemata
are not collapsed. God enacts his intention; Jesus enacts his intention.

The application of the intention-action schema makes clear the
distinction between God and Jesus — each is an agent of intentional
action. While the narrative compels us to say that Jesus is the manifestation of God's action (forcing us to intermingle the schemata), nothing
in that elucidation compels or permits the collapsing of the intention-
action schema, in terms of which both God and Jesus enact their identity, and thus their differentiation as distinct agents of intended actions
is maintained.[13] While Jesus' self-focused identity is enacted by his
holding together, as agent, his powerlessness and power in the transition from death to resurrection, he is utterly dependent upon God, as
agent, to raise him. And while God, and God alone, is the agent who
raises Jesus from the dead, God's intention and action, that is, his
identity, is manifested only in Jesus (the agent who holds together his
own self-focused identity), and thus the identification of God and Jesus
is maintained. Frei thinks it unlikely that a scrutiny of the narratives
will permit us to say more about the unification and distinction between
God and Jesus; nor, of course, does he think we should say less.

While more is not to be observed about the unification and
distinction between God and Jesus in the resurrection narratives, Frei
thinks more is said about Jesus' identity in them. It is in the resurrection
narratives, according to Frei's reading, that Jesus is most fully manifest
as the individual, Jesus of Nazareth. In stage one of the gospel story
(infancy narratives), Jesus is entirely a representative figure. In stage
two (ministry), he is more identified by the kingdom of God than it by
him. In the third stage (passion and resurrection), he emerges as the
unsubstitutable Jesus of Nazareth. "Who is this man? He is Jesus of
Nazareth who, as this man and no other, is truly manifest as the Saviour,
the presence of God" (pp. 136-37).[14]

Certainly a careful reading of the resurrection narrative will not
regard it as myth. For the narrative "concerns an unsubstitutable individual whose mysterious identity is not ineffably behind the story

13. Nor is the self-manifestation schema collapsed by its intermingling with
the intention-action schema in the elucidation of the third stage of the Gospel
narrative.
14. Savior — for he holds together the need of redemption and redemption.

but is inseparable from the unsubstitutable events constituting it, with the resurrection as its climax" (p. 140). The account of the figure and the events that constitute his identity are, in the third stage of the gospel story, so specific and so unlike myth that the reader is very nearly compelled to ask, "Did this actually take place?" (p. 140). In the passion-resurrection sequence "we are confronted with . . . [an] unsubstitutable individual who is what he does and undergoes and is manifested directly as who he is" (p. 143). If fact claims are to be made, they will have to be made about this part of the story. This part of the Gospel account, however, is more nearly fictional than historical in narration; it has about it the fiction writer's direct knowledge of his subject. "Yet the story is about an individual who lived" (p. 144).

> At the crucial climax [of the Gospel narrative, namely the episode] of the resurrection, fictional description, providing direct knowledge of [Jesus'] identity in, with and through the circumstances, merges with factual claim. . . . The narration is at once intensely serious and historical in intent and fictional in form, the common strand between them being the identification of the individual in his circumstances. To know *who* he is in connection with what took place is to know *that* he is. This is the climax of the story and its claim. What the accounts are saying, in effect, is that the being and identity of Jesus in the resurrection are such that his nonresurrection becomes inconceivable. (P. 145)

To grasp Jesus' identity "is to believe that he has been, *in fact*, raised from the dead" (p. 145). For Jesus' identity as the presence of God is identical with his factual existence. How can he who is "the resurrection and the life" be conceived as not resurrected?[15] "The passion-resurrection account tends to force the question of factuality because the claim is involved as part of the very identity that is described as enacted and manifest in the story-event sequence" (p. 146).[16] Who Jesus is is inseparable from the fact that he is. Frei takes this to be the significance of the

---

15. Frei acknowledges that putting the matter in this way leaves out of account more than a little. If Jesus' identity and being cannot be thought apart, then the apprehension of his presence is also unique. "Of what other fact can we say that complete commitment is a way of taking note of it?" (p. 146).

16. Frei interjects the question of how one might answer affirmatively the question of the factuality of the resurrection and suggests that one might replicate the movement of the authors of the Gospels, in which grateful commitment to Jesus and factual affirmation about him were the same act. But he draws back from this

words of the two men spoken to the women at Jesus' tomb, "Why do you seek the living among the dead?" (Luke 24:5), that is, as if it were inconceivable to think of him who lives as among the dead. (A parallel appears in the Fourth Gospel, where Jesus is spoken of as life, *the* life. How can he be conceived as dead?) The recollection of Jesus' prophecy about his death and resurrection with which the two men continue their declaration to the women is "designed to focus [Jesus'] identity as one who lives, who is life and not death. Jesus lives as the one who cannot *not* live, for whom to be what he is is to be" (p. 148). And the one who lives is unambiguously the man, Jesus of Nazareth — the one who was delivered into the hands of sinful men, to be crucified and to rise again. "The prophecy (here taken as fulfilled) is the content of his identity as the one who lives" (p. 148). The statement *that* he is is integral in the statement of *who* he is.

Frei draws a parallel here with Exodus 3:14-15. God directs Moses to tell the people that "I AM" had sent him to them. And then God adds, "Say this to the people Israel, 'The Lord, the God of your fathers, the God of Abraham, the God of Isaac, and the God of Jacob, has sent me to you.'" "For [God] to be and to be this specific one are the same. Similarly, for Jesus to be and to be Jesus the Son of Man and Israel's redeemer are one and the same thing. The ambiguity is over. He, the Christ, can now interpret to them 'in all the scriptures the things concerning himself.' *That* he is and *who* he is — Jesus of Nazareth who, as that one man, is the redeemer undergoing in obedience all that constitutes the climax and summation of Israel's history — are one and the same thing" (p. 149).

*In nuce,* it belongs to Jesus' identity to be alive; who he is has ingredient in it the fact that he lives. Frei's elucidation of the gospel story, with its particular concentration upon the third stage, is circular: The resurrection in manifesting the unsubstitutable man Jesus, in his enacted identity, as the presence of God, manifests Jesus as Savior. To know Jesus in this identity is to believe him present, since the Savior is life, is one who lives. To say that the procedure is circular is not to charge it with a fault.[17] Frei clarifies the logic of the gospel story. His exposition is both cogent and definite to this point. And the definiteness is extended when

---

remark with the statement that he has gone afield, "for it constitutes a reflection concerning the possibility of making the transition from literary description to historical and religious affirmation" (p. 147). His restraint is admirable. It is only that the narrative of the resurrection depicts Jesus overcoming the confusion and doubts of the disciples, and this is a hermeneutical clue not to be omitted.

17. Cf. Frei, *Identity,* pp. 5-9.

he comments that Jesus, who lives and is present, has such a specific, self-focused identity that he can bring it to bear as the identifying clue for his community, which becomes focused by and through him. But indefiniteness begins when he says, "the New Testament will ask just this of all men: To identify themselves by relation . . . to Jesus of Nazareth, who has identified himself with them and for them" (p. 149). This is too general and indefinite a statement. It is true that the New Testament attests that the unsubstitutable Jesus came, died for, and was raised for many. But unsubstitutably ingredient in his coming, intercession, and manifestation are Jesus' appointment, calling, and commissioning of the apostles. This was the manner of his relation to men and he required of these men that they perform their appointment, calling, and commissioning. And by way of their performance, he appoints, calls, and commissions many and requires of many that they identify themselves by *this* relation to him. It is in these terms that Jesus in unsubstitutable fashion identified and identifies himself with human beings and required and requires them to identify themselves with him.

Frei extends his too indefinite account of Jesus' relation to human beings and their relation to Jesus in his discussion of Jesus' presence now, which we examined in Chapter Three. Before he undertakes that discussion, he asks — in concluding his commentary on Jesus' resurrection — what kind of affirmation about the factuality of the resurrection is involved if one believed in Jesus' resurrection. I will conclude this section by attending to his reply to this question.

Frei needs to address this question, because, while he wishes to speak of Christ's presence, he has concentrated on the descriptive structure of the gospel story and not on the question of its factuality. His reply to the question about the factuality of the resurrection of Jesus is made, not surprisingly then, in terms of "the inspired quality of the accounts" (p. 150). The introduction of this phrase is critical to the comparison to be made between Frei and Barth. I have attempted to show that for Barth, the descriptive structure of the gospel story is an exponent of the gathering, upholding, and sending of the apostles; therefore, the gospel story is to be read as a function of this gathering, upholding, and sending. Since Frei has scarcely spoken of the apostles at all, his elucidation of "the inspired quality of the accounts" will be different.

Frei contends that if one believes in the resurrection of Jesus then "at one point a judgment of faith concerning the inspiration of the descriptive contents [of the Gospel account] and a judgment of faith affirming their factual claim would have to coincide" (p. 150). The believer will have to affirm that the writers of the Gospels were more nearly correct to think of Jesus as factually raised, bodily raised, than not to think of him in that way. Frei is not employing excessively cautious language here, but rather is guarding against the attempt to conceive the resurrection directly. The Gospel writers are right to think "more nearly . . . than not" of Jesus as factually raised, since it belongs to Jesus' identity, as Savior, to be factually alive and not dead. And so it is just at this point in the passion-resurrection narrative that, for the believer, a transition is made from literary description to historical-factual and theological judgment.

Why does Frei introduce the term *inspiration* at this point? No evidence for the resurrection can be proffered other than the gospel story itself. Either what is said in the passion-resurrection sequence is true or it is not. Since the material is realistic or "history-like" narrative and not myth, the factual question is pertinent and not irrelevant. While no evidence beyond the story itself can be adduced in support of the factuality of the resurrection, reliable historical evidence against the resurrection would be decisive. "In other words, if the resurrection is true, it is unique, but if false, it is like any other purported fact that has been proved false: there is nothing unique about it in that case. Until such evidence comes along, however, it seems proper to say that there is a kind of logic in a Christian's faith that forces him to say that disbelief in the resurrection of Jesus is rationally impossible" (p. 151). Put positively, a Christian's faith in the resurrection is a matter of faith and not of evidence or speculation.

Barth would not disagree with this statement of Frei's. It is only that he gives a definite content to inspiration, where Frei, whose language remains formal, scarcely does. According to Barth's exposition, even as the apostles were gathered and upheld and sent by Jesus, so Jesus, in the power of the Spirit, includes many in the knowledge and with the persons of the apostles in this movement. Frei, by concentrating on Jesus' enacted identity in relation to God and on its manifestation by the act of God, but scarcely at all on Jesus' enacted identity in relation to the apostles and the confirmation of *that* identity by the act of God, leaves out of account the apostles' identity — and ours, too, as participant in the apostles' identity. (It is this relationship of Jesus with the apostles and the apostles with Jesus, and the participation of many in this definite relationship, that Barth denominates *inspiration*.) Thus, for Frei *inspiration* is an abstract affirmation of the truth of the gospel story, coordinate with a placing of ourselves in the gospel story and the whole biblical story, howbeit by the power of the Holy Spirit.

Yet we should acknowledge that Frei "scarcely" regards Jesus' relationship with the apostles, rather than "not at all." In the introduction to his commentary on the Gospels (Part II), where Frei already indicates that the individual, specific, unsubstitutable identity of Jesus is most fully set forth in the account of his resurrection appearances, he includes this remark: "The focusing of [Jesus'] full identity in the resurrection is what enables him to turn and share his presence with his disciples" (p. 49). Frei does not develop this point. He approaches the point again in the "Meditation" he appends to *Identity*. There Frei writes, "[Jesus'] cross and his resurrection are a secret place all his own, for they leave behind every common medium, every comparison by which we know things" (p. 172). Jesus in his death and resurrection, in his relationship to God, is inaccessible to us. Yet, while a veil remains between Jesus and us, the passion-resurrection sequence tells of one who embraces both sides of the veil. To elucidate this point, Frei cites a passage from Schweitzer, which he regards as a true account of the way the Easter story becomes a truth for us: "[Jesus] comes to us as One unknown, without a name, as of old, by the lake-side, He came to those men who knew him not. He speaks to us the same word: 'Follow thou me!' and sets us to the tasks which He has to fulfil for our time. He commands. And to those who obey Him, whether they be wise or simple, He will reveal Himself in the toils, conflicts, the sufferings which they shall have to pass through in His fellowship, and, as an ineffable mystery, they shall learn in their own experience Who He is."[18]

Frei approaches a description of Jesus' relationship with the apostles as the constituting and definite shape of his relationship with "us," but does not cross over into the description of it, which is so critical in Barth's exposition.

## Conclusion

### Barth

Barth begins his discussion of Jesus' death by observing the contrast in the Gospels between the account of his death and the account of his

---

18. Albert Schweitzer, *The Quest of the Historical Jesus* (New York, 1956), p. 403; cited in Frei, *Identity*, p. 171.

ministry. Jesus demonstrates the kingdom of God in his ministry of word and act. And the disciples are appointed witnesses of this demonstration. It is integral to the passion story that it be preceded by Jesus' demonstration of the kingdom of God to the disciples and followed by the dumbfounding of the disciples. A literary or dramatic element is present in the sequence; the dumbfounding of the disciples makes it evident that the passion of Jesus is not self-evidently the end and fulfillment of Jesus' ministry.

But a deeper element is also present. Although the disciples are appointed witnesses of Jesus' ministry, they cannot perform this task on the basis of their appointment alone. On the basis of their appointment alone they are unable to recognize Jesus' death as the aim and goal of his ministry. More precisely, it belongs to the witness of the apostles to attest that on the basis of their appointment alone they are unable to recognize the light of Jesus' ministry to be the one true Light. On the basis of their appointment they see only an absurd future to Jesus' ministry in his death, a future in which the disobedient triumph and the genuine benefactor dies as a criminal.

What is it that enables the apostles to recognize the light of his ministry as the one true Light? It is, of course, the resurrection that *manifests* to the disciples the secret of Jesus' ministry. But in his exposition Barth first refers to the "striking passage" of John 17:19-20a: "For their sake I consecrate myself, that they also may be consecrated in truth. I do not pray for these only, but also for those who believe in me through their word." While the fact that Jesus has upheld, upholds, and will uphold the disciples is *manifested* to them in Jesus' resurrection from the dead, the fact of the upholding is what Jesus performs in his passion and death for them. It is when the apostle recognizes that "the Son of God loved me and gave Himself for me" that he receives his calling and can attest the light of Jesus' ministry as the one true Light for him and for many (or all).

Barth reads the Gospels as attesting that Jesus' ministry is directed toward his death. He attempts to demonstrate this under four points, which I will examine in turn. (1) Jesus appointed Judas to be an apostle. He did this knowing what Judas would do. We have seen earlier that, according to Barth, the Gospels depict Judas as a representative of the Twelve. By virtue of their appointment the Twelve did not become righteous, no longer sinners. They were and continued to be sinners. It is only that Christ's death upholds them, sinners, by keeping them in relationship with him, calling them to proclaim, from the event of his relationship with them, his ministry and death for them and, by way of their word, for many. (Even Judas is made to serve the purpose of his appointment and calling, although negatively, while Paul is called and commissioned to fulfill Judas' appointment and calling positively.) While the death of Christ is the upholding of all, its definiteness is founded in his upholding of the apostles.

(2) Jesus was "delivered up by the determinate counsel and foreknowledge of God" (Acts 2:23). The direction of "the determinate counsel" of God is delineated in the Fourth Gospel.[19]

> Father, the hour has come; glorify the Son that the Son may glorify thee, since thou hast given him power over all flesh, so that he might give eternal life to all whom thou hast given him. And this is eternal life, that they know thee the only true God, and Jesus Christ whom thou has sent. . . . I have manifested thy name to the men whom thou gavest me out of the world; thine they were, and thou gavest them to me, and they have kept thy word. Now they know that everything that thou hast given me is from thee; for I have given them the words which thou gavest me, and they have received them and know in truth that I come from thee; and they believed that thou didst send me. I am praying for them; I am not praying for the world but for those whom thou hast given me, for they are thine. . . . While I was with them, I kept them in thy name which thou hast given me; I have guarded them, and none of them is lost but the son of perdition, that the scripture might be fulfilled. . . . Consecrate them in the truth; thy word is truth. As thou didst send me into the world, so I have sent them into the world. And for their sake I consecrate myself, that they also may be consecrated in truth. I do not pray for these only, but also for those who are to believe in me through their word. (John 17:1-20)

Barth does not render a full exposition of this text. He does not, for example, sort out how Jesus has kept and keeps the apostles in his word despite all of their deafness, dumbfoundedness, and confusion. He only refers back to this text (John 17) in his commentary on Peter's declaration that Jesus was delivered up to death by "the determinate counsel"

19. Barth, in elucidating Acts 2:23, says that he does not need to return to the emphasis on δεῖ in the passion narratives, which he had examined a few pages earlier, "although it is here primarily that this point is substantiated" (C.D. IV/2, p. 260). In his exposition of δεῖ (pp. 255ff.) Barth refers to John's Gospel (esp. chap. 17).

of God. The reference provides Barth with the answer to the question, Why did God will to deliver up Jesus and cause Jesus to be delivered up to death? That Jesus might be consecrated as Intercessor, the Intercessor for the apostles and for those who believe the word of the apostles.[20] Even in his account of God's agency in delivering up Jesus to death, Barth finds it necessary to emphasize Jesus' relationship with the apostles.

(3) It is Israel which delivered up Jesus, rejected him, and condemned him to death. Integral to the passion story "is the riddle of the existence of Israel in its relationship to Jesus" (p. 261). The delivering up of Jesus to death by Israel is foreshadowed in his rejection in his hometown, in the rain of objections to his activities, in the questions about his authority, in the attempts to "catch him in his words," in accusations that his power was of the devil, in plots against him, in the hostility of the authorities. What is foreshadowed eventuates in Jesus being delivered up by the Jews to the Gentile authorities. This "'handing over' of Jesus on the morning of Good Friday was the founding of the Church as a Church of both Jews and Gentiles, and therefore as a missionary Church" (p. 263).

Jesus in his exaltation commissioned the apostles to be his witnesses to the end of the earth. But the commission is not conferred without positive and negative anticipations. The apostolic story, according to Barth's exposition of it, describes the apostolic handing over of Jesus to the Gentiles as a replication of Israel's handing over of Jesus to the Gentiles. The missionary character of the apostolate, and of the subsequent Christian community in replication of it, is not a matter of indefiniteness, but is specifically shaped by Jesus' death, including Israel's initiative and participation in it.

---

20. Hoskyns makes the following comment on John 17:19, "[The Death of Jesus] is an effective sacrifice because Jesus by His Word made it to be so, and it is an effective sacrifice for His disciples only, because the consecrating word was spoken in their presence only and on their behalf only. The Death of Jesus is effective for the world only in so far as it believes in Him, and receives and accepts His consecrating Word, since it is this consecrating word, not the murderous activity of the [crucifiers], that makes His death an effective and redemptive act." E. C. Hoskyns, *The Fourth Gospel*, ed. F. N. Davey (London, 1967), p. 502.

Hoskyns also notes that the Greek word ἁγιάζειν, rendered "consecrate" in English, is used in the Septuagint in the context of the sacrifice ceremonies. In relation to Jesus, in John 17, it means "I offer myself a sacrifice." The beneficiary of the sacrifice is the apostolate, not for its own sake, but rather that it may serve the truth in and for the world (pp. 502-4).

Barth places the riddle of the existence of the apostolate in parallel with the riddle of the existence of Israel. Israel first, then the prophets within Israel, then the apostolate, and then the Church of Jews and Gentiles are appointed and called. Scripture is the account of the Lord's appointment and calling of these witnesses and of the obedience and disobedience to their appointment and calling of these witnesses. All others are appointed and called by way of or in consonance with Scripture's narration of the appointment and calling of these witnesses. Moreover, Israel was not only gathered (appointed) and called (upheld); it was provisionally sent ("to be a light to lighten the Gentiles"). At the point when its sending is no longer to be provisional but is to be fulfilled, it executes its commission negatively. It says No to it, rather than Yes. Following upon this No, the apostolate receives its commission from the Messiah of Israel; and accepting it and his calling (his upholding), it executes positively Israel's commission. In his account of Israel's rejection of Christ, Barth finds it necessary to emphasize Jesus' relationship with his apostles.

(4) "The determination of the existence of Jesus for death . . . has in the existence of the disciples a counterpart" (p. 263). The disciples are a counterpart because their calling, by and for which Jesus frees them, is neither formless nor something to which they have to provide the form. The definite form and direction of Jesus' existence gives definite form and direction to the existence of the apostles. This is the case because Jesus' call binds a human to himself. Barth takes care to distinguish the primary *theologia crucis* of the Gospels from the secondary. But the secondary *theologia crucis*, that of the disciples, cannot be separated from the primary. "If the word 'discipleship' is in any way used to denote something general and not a concrete and therefore concretely filled out happening between Jesus and this particular man, the command 'Follow me' can only be described as quite meaningless. For the only possible content of this command is that this . . . specific man to whom it is given should come to, follow, and be with the One who gives it. . . . That . . . is the one complete work he is called to do" (p. 536). This specific man who is a sinner, and has to suffer the consequences, is called to rely upon the One who calls him, to rely upon his intercession as the sole supporting ground on which to stand and to suffer the consequences. Of course he is unable to do this except as Jesus grants him the freedom (power) to do so.

What is of special pertinence for our study is to observe how Barth establishes the point that while the primary *theologia crucis* must be distinguished from the secondary, the two cannot be separated. Jesus, consenting to his death and suffering it, *obeyed* the will of the Father who determined death as the goal of his Son's life. Jesus calls the apostles to *obey* him (who is one with the Father), to consent to being conformed to his life determined for death, which conforming is their calling.[21] It is not possible to speak of the death of Christ without speaking of Jesus' relationship with his apostles. Ingredient in his consenting to and suffering his death, in obedience to the Father, is his (accomplished) intention that the goal of his life, intercessory death, become and be the ground of his upholding (calling) of his apostles and, by way of their witness, of many (or all).

I now turn to Barth's commentary on Jesus' resurrection and ascension. Everything in the New Testament either looks forward to the forty days (the first two stages of the Gospels) or back to them (Acts, the Epistles, the Apocalypse). Jesus in the resurrection appearances does not have a changed form of existence; these appearances are the manifestation of the man Jesus who performed deeds and preached in Galilee and was crucified in Jerusalem. The very word *manifestation* implicates the apostles. They were in need of it. How could they proclaim a Jesus whose identity was hidden from them by the appearance of ignominy, despicability, and insignificance? In his resurrection appearances, Jesus communicates effectively to the apostles who he is. For in communicating to them that he is, he communicates to them that he who was dead lives; that the One who had demonstrated the kingdom of God in word and act and suffered death in that demonstration lives. And in communicating to them who he is, he communicates that he has the freedom (power) to communicate himself to them, to make himself, so inaccessible otherwise, known to them. He gave them the ground for all they would think and say of him. And not only the ground, but the power (freedom) — for how would they now not speak of him to Israel and the Gentiles? Jesus' manifestation in his resurrection is the effective instruction of the apostles. Barth refers to the "manifestation" as the decisive factor in the gospel story.

To say that Jesus' manifestation is the decisive factor in the gospel story is not to diminish stages one and two, the accounts of his

---

21. The apostolic conformation to Christ's life determined for death is always, in Barth's exposition, first the upholding of the apostles. It removes them from the death he vanquished. Second, it is their task, to witness in act and speech to the freedom from death in a world threatened by it. Only threatened!

ministry and passion. The manifestation of Jesus' identity to the apostles illumines the first two stages and brings into unity all three stages. Its light kindles the lights of the earlier episodes and integrates them with itself. The apostles were appointed to attest to Jesus' ministry of word and act. But they did not recognize in his ministry *the* Light. They were called to confess him, but did not yet rely upon him alone. In the gospel account the disciples are so dependent on the manifestation of Jesus in his resurrection that every event of Jesus' relationship with them is depicted as an anticipation of his effective self-communication to them. And the manifestation is attested, in the apostolic story, as perfect, in the sense that it is never replaced. The final Parousia will be the same manifestation. Nor is it replaced by the coming of the Holy Spirit. Wherever Jesus is known by the witness of the Holy Spirit, "it is always in the glory in which he was then manifested to the disciples and known by them" (p. 142). His manifestation in the resurrection was, is, and will be sufficient for all times. "This is the objective basis from which alone, by the witness of the Holy Spirit, all subjective knowledge of Jesus Christ can derive — the knowledge of the disciples, the first community and the later Church" (p. 142).

In observing that in the gospel narrative the resurrection-ascension is described as an event in the world of space and time, and not merely as an inner experience of the disciples, Barth draws attention to the particular emphasis laid upon Jesus' being seen, heard, and touched by the disciples during the forty days. Attending to this emphasis, Barth makes two points. First, as an event in Jesus' existence, it was a concrete event in the disciples' existence. Second, it was the event that effectively changed the disciples' relationship with Jesus.

While both points are critical, the second is given special elaboration. In the forty days, it was Jesus' acting with the apostles as he had acted with them before, but now in the power of his manifestation, that changed the apostles' relationship with him. Whether or not they recognize him in a way that is effective for them is not in the hands of the apostles, but rather is in Jesus' hands. It is Jesus who gives them the freedom (power) to recognize that the One who is now alive and with them is he who was with them in Galilee and Jerusalem and had gone to his death. Who Jesus was for the disciples, the One who appointed and called them — he, in his resurrection, manifests that he is and always will be for them. And since he sends them to the end of the earth, who he is and always will be for them, he also is and will be for all — the One who appointed and called the disciples. The resurrection-ascension is the event in which Jesus shares himself, in the fullness of his enacted identity, with the apostles. While this event is incomprehensible, in that Jesus' resurrection from the dead is an act of God, the apostles have knowledge of it through Jesus' sharing of his knowledge with them. "Because it is an event which took place for the apostles in their encounter with the living Christ, the knowledge of it [and of Jesus' identity manifested in it] will necessarily be ordered by their witness and continually be orientated by it" (p. 149).

In his resurrection appearances Jesus came to the apostles. "Where did He come from?" Barth asks. He had come to them earlier, during his ministry. He was recognized by them then, for they followed him. But he was not recognized fully by them, for they were not irrevocably bound to him. What totally concealed him from them was his death. They could not recognize him as "the lamb of God which takes away the sin of the world." Their appointment was not binding and their calling was unrecognized. When he comes to them *from* death and *from* his awakening from the dead,[22] they recognize who it was who had demonstrated the kingdom of God in word and act — the King; and they recognized who it was who had been put to death — the One who is redeemed from death, the One who has power over death, namely, the Redeemer. They are effectively, irrevocably, constituted subjects of this King (not merely pupils of this teacher), conscious recipients of his power over death, and knowers of his identity who cannot be or be kept quiet about him, being made lights by his illumination. In sum, they are effectively appointed, called, and commissioned.

When Jesus left his apostles, where did he go? Barth finds two answers in the gospel account. (1) To a place inaccessible to humans. (2) To the place of rule in his fellowship with God. Jesus is inaccessible to humans. He was inaccessible to the apostles until he shared himself in his self-focused identity with them in the resurrection. In the resurrection he shared himself only with his disciples. His manner of sharing himself (since his identity and mission coincide) may be denominated by the word *commissioning*, as long as it comprehends the making effective of *appointment* and *calling*. Of all humans, then, it is only to the apostles that Jesus, in his resurrection, makes himself accessible.

But this same unsubstitutable Jesus is the One who wills to rule and does rule all humans and "desires all humans to come to the knowledge of the truth" (1 Tim. 2:4). Jesus, who in the first place effectively

---

22. This is Barth's twofold answer to the question, Whence?

appoints, calls, and commissions the apostles, now, from his inaccessible place of rule, appoints, calls, and commissions all humans by way of his appointment, calling, and commissioning of the apostles. The gathering, upholding, and sending of the apostles by Christ and their entry into this movement is, on both sides, the movement or event by which Christ rules over all humans and over the whole cosmos. This movement — of Christ gathering, upholding, and sending and of his disciples coming together, confessing, and going forth — is in the first place the movement by which the witness of his apostles is held together; then it is the movement by which their witness is held together with the witness of the prophets; then it is the movement into which the church, by the replication enjoined upon it, is brought and held together; finally it is the movement into which all flesh is being and shall be brought and held together.[23]

## Frei

I will first signal Frei's inattention to Jesus' relationship with the apostles in his exposition of the gospel story's account of the death of Christ and then examine it more closely. (1) Frei speaks about Jesus' obedience to the Father. But he does not say much about the interconnection of Jesus' act of intentional obedience to the Father with Jesus' demand that the apostles obey him, or even, explicitly, with Jesus' upholding of the apostles. (2) Frei speaks about Jesus holding together power and powerlessness. Jesus' very powerlessness is his power to substitute his death for that of others. But Frei does not speak of Jesus' powerlessness as the empowering of the otherwise powerless apostolate. (3) Frei observes that in the gospel story Jesus becomes genuinely powerless. He delivers himself and is delivered into the hands of men, who increasingly restrict his liberty of action until he cannot act at all. But Frei does not advert to the complicity of Jesus' disciples in his being delivered; that is, to Judas' betrayal, Peter's denial, the sleep of the disciples who could not watch and wait. (4) Frei, with a subtlety demanded by the texts, examines Jesus' relation to God. He carefully exposits the explicit and scarcely explicit texts that indicate that Jesus was delivered up by "the determinate counsel" of God. But he does not attend to the point that it is the apostolate that is, in the first place, the beneficiary of Christ's sacrifice — a sacrifice willed by God; a point observed by Barth and even more clearly by Hoskyns.

I will now examine each of these points by way of a brief devel-

---

23. This understanding governs Barth's reading of Scripture.

opment of them. (1) Frei refers to Jesus' obedience as obedience to his mission. And while he uses the phrase as an indicator of Jesus' relation to the One who sent him, he also comments that the emphasis in the Gospels on *mission* signifies that the center of Jesus' person is not in himself but in relation to the persons he encounters. It is only that he does not specify that these persons are, often and critically, the disciples. Frei even observes that Jesus' obedience to God "provides a clue to the New Testament's understanding of how others are to see their own identity in relation to that of Jesus" (p. 108). But he does not elaborate on the comment by any reference to the apostle's identity as one gathered, upheld, and sent or to Jesus as the Gatherer, Upholder, and Sender.

(2) In his account of Jesus' power and powerlessness, Frei elucidates the pattern of exchange drawn from Deutero-Isaiah and used by the Gospel writers in their description of Jesus. In it the coexistence of power and powerlessness is made evident. Jesus' very power exists in his powerlessness to act for himself. But the intertwining of Jesus' power and powerlessness with the powerlessness and power of the apostles, such as we saw exhibited in Barth's account of the calling of the apostles, is not present in Frei's account.

(3) Frei comments, in his elucidation of Jesus' transition from power to powerlessness, that "the transition is effected through [Jesus'] own decision, as well as through the action of the authorities" (p. 113). Barth thinks it critical to stress the disciples' complicity in the transition. If Peter is "the prince of the apostles," Barth writes, he is so in the sense of leading them in defection. And another representative apostle, Judas, expresses in concentrated, if less intentionally violent, form precisely the intention enacted by the Jewish authorities. The point Barth makes is not so much that no apostle stands as an apostle by his own power, but, more deeply, that Jesus is contradicted by his apostles so that his death is, in the first place, his contradiction of their contradiction and therein the upholding of the apostles as apostles. Again, the omission of any significant mention of the apostles by Frei is not to be criticized merely on the grounds that an oversight appears in his exposition. Rather, if the Gospels recount the passion of Jesus as the calling (upholding) of the disciples, his ministry as the appointment (gathering) of the disciples, and his manifestation as the commissioning (sending) of his disciples, then the texts are the exponents of this movement, this movement being the one into which those who come after the disciples, and by way of their word, are drawn by Jesus. This has a critical bearing on the way in which these texts are to be read.

(4) While the gospel story's account of the interrelation of Jesus and the Father belongs, obviously, to the passion story, it does so, Frei indicates, only as that interrelation is manifested in Jesus' resurrection. I will turn, then, to Frei's commentary on the gospel account of Jesus' resurrection, only reiterating for the moment that when Frei does eluci-date the Gospels' description of this interrelation he does not consider the point that the beneficiary of Jesus' God-willed sacrifice is, in the first place, the apostolate.

The pattern of the interrelation of Jesus (his intention and action) and God (his intention and action), which Frei elucidates, is embedded in the passion-resurrection sequence of the Synoptic Gospels. In the resurrection God, and God alone, acts; Jesus, and Jesus alone, appears. Jesus — in his enacted identity — is the manifestation of the presence of God's action. God is the one who enacts this manifestation.[24] Both Jesus and God are active agents (although their interrelation as active agents is irreducibly complex in the narrative), but while Jesus identifies himself with God's intention by making its enactment his intention, it is God's act that manifests God's identification with Jesus.

One might expect Frei, at this point, simply to say that God manifests Jesus as the presence of his activity. While Frei does say that, he also says that Jesus' identity becomes so self-focused in the passion-resurrection narrative sequence that he can turn and share who he is with others. While the terminology of Frei and Barth is different, there is no reason to seek a great difference between them at this point. Moreover, one may assume that when Frei says that the man Jesus, now identified as Savior, can turn and share his self-focused presence with others, he means, in the first place, with the disciples. But while con-centrating on Jesus' identity as Savior in the passion-resurrection sequence, Frei, having left out of account Jesus as Gatherer and Upholder of the disciples (in the earlier stages) and Sender of the disciples (in this third stage), cannot specify the definite shape of Jesus' sharing himself with the apostles. While Frei scarcely leaves out of account Jesus as Savior and salvation, he does omit any development of the terms *Savior* and *salvation* according to their persistent, concrete shape throughout the gospel narrative.

Frei is careful to distance the resurrection narrative from myth. The Jesus who is raised is an unsubstitutable person, and unsubstitut-able character and incident are not the stuff of myth. This leads Frei to

24. Here Frei intermingles his identity description schemata.

observe that since the passion-resurrection narrative is "history-like" and about an individual who lived, we are very nearly compelled to ask if these events actually took place. And Frei does not avoid a reply to the question. For the person who believes with the story that Jesus is Savior, Jesus' not being factually raised becomes inconceivable. The reasoning is stringent. And while formal, it is not without reference to content — the continuity of Jesus' identity in the transitions from power to powerlessness and from powerlessness to power. Yet in this a critical unsubstitutability is overlooked. Jesus underwent these transitions with and for certain specific men. His proclamation in word and act took place in front of them; his death was for them; his resurrection appearances were to them. They attest that he appointed, called, and commissioned them. What Frei says about Jesus' identity — its manifestation being the content of the resurrection narrative — is consonant with the texts. Yet what Frei says not only does not say enough but, more specifically, does not say enough about how the texts are to be read. For what he leaves out has to do with their "historical" character. Their "historical" character refers to more than the historical factuality of Jesus' resurrection.

Barth signifies that the texts provide "historical" knowledge in two senses. First, an investigation of the texts will not seek alleged historical facts behind the texts, but will investigate the historical texts themselves. Frei, as far as he goes, concurs. But what does Barth mean by "historical texts"? He means that while they speak of Jesus' ministry, death, and resurrection they speak of these events as the events of the apostles being gathered, upheld, and sent. The New Testament texts, while describing the movement of Jesus through his ministry, passion, and resurrection to his ascension, are themselves exponents of the described participation of the apostles in each of these events, denominated by the terms *appointment, calling,* and *commissioning.* And the Jesus who appointed, called, and commissioned the disciples in this movement appoints, calls, and commissions those who hear their word in or from the texts that describe this movement. As long as the texts are not recognized to have this "historical" character, a "mythologizing" of salvation is invited, even in face of the unsubstitutable Savior, as incoherent as the result will be.

Second, an investigation that recognizes the "historical" character of the texts will be impartial. It will not fit them into some picture of the world and history. Again, Frei, as far as he goes, would concur.[25]

---

25. And he goes far, as the whole conception of *Eclipse* testifies.

But Barth goes further. If we allow the New Testament texts to say what they intend to say and do say, our interpretive procedure will follow their own procedure. Our explication and application of all of the texts of the Gospels, and consequently those of Acts, the Epistles, and the Apocalypse, will be an explication and application of the movement out of which the texts come and which they describe as such, and in which they ever cohere. And the Old Testament texts will be explicated and applied as the gathering, upholding, and provisional sending of Israel. Frei's account of what we have called "living in the Word" is altogether helpful, but it is the literary ancilliary to and development of the "historical" movement of the gathering, upbuilding, and sending of the apostolate and the anticipation of this movement in the gathering, upbuilding, and provisional sending of Israel. While Frei's attention to the question of the historical factuality of Jesus' resurrection is significant and helpful, attention to the historical character of the New Testament texts is, at minimum, as important.[26]

Frei, in a clear and cogent exposition of the gospel story, puts such an emphasis on Jesus' holding together his identity as crucified and risen, that it is surprising that he makes virtually no reference to those to whom and for whom Jesus enacted this holding together of his identity. It is to certain men that Christ interprets "in all scripture the things concerning himself." As Jesus holds together his identity as the demonstrator of the kingdom, the crucified One and the risen One in front of the disciples, he demands that they hold together their identity as the appointed, called, and commissioned — hold together this identity and no other. And, as must always be said, he demands this of them because his identity *effects* their appointment, calling, and commissioning and thereby makes it possible. Again, his power is the power of their possibility; otherwise they are powerless. It is this relationship of Jesus with his apostles, so definitely described in the text, to which we apply the term *historical* to distinguish this definite rela-

---

26. The "historical" character of the texts, again, does not have reference to alleged facts behind the text. The texts are exponents of the appointment, calling, and commissioning of the apostles. The texts describe this threefold movement. The believer affirms that the apostles were chosen in this threefold way, for his own threefold chosenness is participant in theirs. With regard to the factuality of this movement, the believer can only say that the pupil is not above his teacher — here the apostles being the teachers; teachers by virtue of their own pupilship. Barth is careful not to describe the apostles as mediators of Christ to us. Rather, they teach to us their living relationship with Christ, in which only Christ makes us participant.

tionship of Jesus with his disciples from any indefinite account of a relation between Jesus and others. But the use of the word *historical* needs further elucidation, for just because something is definite or unsubstitutable does not mean, *eo ipso*, that it is historical.

This elucidation may take place in parallel with Frei's reply to the question about the factuality of the resurrection of Jesus. Frei asks what kind of affirmation about the resurrection is involved if one believes in Jesus' resurrection. Frei is so attentive to the descriptive structure of the biblical texts that we would not expect him suddenly to break his concentration and begin to seek for evidence that the resurrection of Jesus did in fact occur. And, of course, he does not do so. What is involved, for someone who believes in Jesus' resurrection, when it comes to affirming that Jesus was in fact raised, is "a belief in something like the inspired quality of the accounts" (p. 150). If one believes that Jesus is the Savior of human beings from death — as the New Testament depicts him — then one can only affirm that Jesus himself, who died, is alive, factually alive in the way in which the New Testament describes — in factual contradiction of the factual death from which he was raised. Either what is said in the passion-resurrection sequence is true or it is not. Since this narrative is not myth, reliable historical evidence against the resurrection would be decisive. So, again, either the text is true or it is not. "A belief in something like the inspired quality of the accounts" is a belief that they reflect what "actually took place."

Barth gives a wider sense and a content to *inspiration*. The New Testament texts describe the gathering, upholding, and sending of the apostles. Belief in inspiration is the belief that the New Testament texts arise out of and ever cohere in this gathering, upholding, and sending of the apostles by Jesus — they are exponents of it. Belief in inspiration is belief that Jesus actually gathered, upheld, and sent these men and continues to gather, uphold, and send many by making these many participant in the threefold chosenness of the apostles. There is a distinction, but no gap, between the text and what it describes in this regard. There is a distinction in that Jesus, and not the text, executes this threefold choosing of many, but there is no gap in that what Jesus does and what the text describes him as doing are one, for Jesus ever utters his own Word as the Word of the appointment, calling, and commissioning of many. Even as in the text he appointed, called, and commissioned the apostles, he appoints, calls, and commissions many (or all) by way of the apostles' testimony to his threefold choosing of them. That is Barth's account of inspiration.

It is not that Frei does not approach this account. He approaches a description of Jesus' relationship with the apostles as the constituting and definite shape of his relationship with us, but he does not cross over into a description of it. And, therefore, his procedure for biblical interpretation is governed more nearly by (what we have called) the pattern of "living in the Word" than by inspiration, our inclusion in the apostolate. To be governed in the procedure of biblical interpretation by inspiration, as we may describe Barth's procedure, means that we not only regard the biblical texts as held together by the threefold movement in which Jesus located and locates the apostles, but also we regard the threefold movement in which Jesus locates the apostles (as described in the text) as the definite, concrete movement in which we, in the fullness of our lives, have been, are, and will be located by Jesus, as he joins together the apostles' mission and our mission in his mission.

# Index of Subjects

Accessibility of Jesus, 29, 30
Apostles. *See* Disciples
Apostolic story, 48-49
Appointment: of the disciples, 5, 9, 97; handing over and, 38-39; of Judas, 34-35; material content of, 38; of Paul, 38, 39, 40
Ascension: to God, 85, 103. *See also* Resurrection-ascension
Awakening, 49

Biblical interpretation: Calvin's method of, 63-64; historical knowledge and, 83-84, 107-8; Holy Spirit and, 63; inspiration and, 110; typology in, 63-64

Calvin, John, 63-64
Central intention, 4
Church: appointment of, 59; birth of, 65; connection to Jesus Christ, 66; constitution of, 45; difference from Jesus, 44; as an event, 49; gathering of, 49; inclusion in the apostolate, 50, 51, 58-60, 65-66; indirect presence of Jesus and, 43-44; intention-action pattern of, 44;

relationship to the apostles, 49-51; task of, 59, 61
Commands: as commands to the church, 58-61; historical particularity of, 52-54, 58; Jesus' work and, 59-60. *See also* Universal principles
Commissioning of the disciples, 7, 17, 18-20, 31-32, 99-100, 103
Common meal, 81-82
Cosmic reconciliation, 72

Death of Jesus: beneficiaries of, 72, 79, 99n, 104, 106; disciples' confusion over, 69-70, 97; as fulfillment of Jesus' life, 70, 72-73, 97-101; God's providence and, 73; Jesus' mission and, 71-72; Jesus' predictions of, 70-71; kingdom of God and, 70-71; patterns of meaning in, 85-86; purpose of, 99; resurrection and, 71; substitution and, 79
Defection, 12, 13
Disciples: appointment of, 5, 9, 34-40, 97; blindness of, 69-70; calling of, 32-34; cleansing of, 35-36; commissioning of, 7, 17, 18-20, 31-32,

**111**

99-100, 103; as defectors, 12-13; empowerment of, 32; freedom of, 66; as gatherers, 9; identification with Jesus, 9-10, 74; identity of, 3, 5, 20-21; Jesus' intention for, 10; participation with Jesus, 5; power and powerlessness of, 12-13, 14-15, 21; proclamation of, 19; relationship to the church, 51; as revealers, 14; righteousness of, 29; shared guilt of, 35; as sinners, 32-33, 97; as witnesses, 76-77. *See also* Relationship of Jesus and the disciples

Discipleship, 100

Explicative reading, 21-23

Figuration, 47, 63-64

Garden of Gethsemane, 11
Gnosticism, 14, 26-30
God: determinate counsel of, 98-99; intention-action of, 15-17, 20, 88, 90-91; relation to Jesus, 46, 90-91; supersession of Jesus, 15-16, 89
Gospel story: apostolic story and, 48; birth of the church in, 65; differences from the savior myth, 27-30, 91-92, 106; factuality of, 92n.16, 94-95, 107, 109; historical character of, 107, 108n; overlapping stages in, 6, 22; patterns in, 8; significance of third stage in, 74-75, 76; stages of, 1-4, 22, 74; themes of, 22; uniqueness of events in, 28; unity of, 47, 102
Great Commission, 7

Handing over, 35, 36-37, 38-40, 99
Hermeneutics, 5-6, 14-15, 22-23
Historical forces, 6-7, 15, 86, 89
Historical knowledge, 83-84, 107
History, 44-45, 47
Holiness, 55

Holy Spirit, 20, 42-43, 46, 49, 63
Hoskyns, E. C., 99n, 104

Identity, 4, 44
Identity of Jesus: anticipations of, 79; common meal and, 81-82; enactment of, 78-79; as Gatherer, 9; identity of disciples and, 108; miracles and, 77; in obedience, 4-5, 7, 8, 10-11, 86-87; as the one who lives, 92-93; perception of, 81, 97; in relationship to the disciples, 20-21; in relationship to God, 20; resurrection and, 16-17, 81, 82, 91-93; as Savior, 10, 79, 106; secret of, 77
Indirect presence of Jesus, 42
Inspiration, 94-95, 109
Intercession of Jesus, 11, 12, 13, 15, 34, 100-101
Israel: appointment and calling of, 100; Jesus Christ and, 1; resistance to Jesus, 73-74, 99

Jesus Christ: accessibility of, 29, 30; contradiction by the disciples, 105; enacted intention of, 6-7, 8, 10; identification with the disciples, 9-10, 74; identification with God, 89; identification with Israel, 1; indirect presence of, 42; intention-action of, 90-91; as the intention-action of God, 16-17, 20; intercession of, 11, 12, 13, 15, 34, 100-101; interrelation with God, 46, 89-91, 106; mission of, 86-87, 105; obedience of, 4, 7-10, 86-87, 104, 105; power and powerlessness of, 10-11, 14-15, 21, 86, 87-88, 104, 105; power of, 17, 19, 60; presence of, 5-6, 20, 42-46, 61-62; public enactments of, 29; redemption of, 16, 90; relation to human beings, 94; as a representative figure, 2; righteousness of, 29;

# Index of Scripture References